HOW TO FORM A NONPROFIT CORPORATION

with forms

HOW TO FORM A NONPROFIT CORPORATION

with forms

Mark Warda
Attorney at Law

SPHINX® PUBLISHING

A Division of Sourcebooks, Inc.®

Naperville, IL

First edition, 2000

Published by: **Sourcebooks, Inc.**®

Naperville Office
P.O. Box 4410
Naperville, Illinois 60567-4410
630-961-3900
Fax: 630-961-2168

Cover Design: Sourcebooks, Inc.®
Interior Design and Production: Amy S. Hall/Mark Warda, Sourcebooks, Inc.®

This publication is designed to provide accurate and authoritative information in regard to the subject matter covered. It is sold with the understanding that the publisher is not engaged in rendering legal, accounting, or other professional service. If legal advice or other expert assistance is required, the services of a competent professional person should be sought.

From a Declaration of Principles Jointly Adopted by a Committee of the
American Bar Association and a Committee of Publishers and Associations

This product is not a substitute for legal advice

Disclaimer required by Texas statutes

Library of Congress Cataloging-in-Publication Data
Warda, Mark.
   How to form a nonprofit corporation : with forms / mark Warda.
      p. cm.
   Includes index.
   ISBN 1-57248-099-8 (pbk.)
      1. Nonprofit organizations--Law and legislation--United Stated--Popular works. 2. Nonprofit organizations--Law and legislation--United States--Forms. I. Title.

KF1388.Z9 W37 2000
346.73'064--dc21

                                                              99-053064

Printed and bound in the United States of America.
HS Paperback — 10 9 8 7 6 5 4 3 2

CONTENTS

USING SELF-HELP LAW BOOKS

Before using a self-help law book, you should realize the advantages and disadvantages of doing your own legal work and understand the challenges and diligence that this requires.

A GROWING TREND

Rest assured that you won't be the first or only person handling your own legal matter. For example, in some states, more than seventy-five percent of the people in divorces and other cases represent themselves. Because of the high cost of legal services, this is a major trend and many courts are struggling to make it easier for people to represent themselves. However, some courts are not happy with people who do not use attorneys and refuse to help them in any way. For some, the attitude is, "Go to the law library and figure it out for yourself."

We write and publish self-help law books to give people an alternative to the often complicated and confusing legal books found in most law libraries. We have made the explanations of the law as simple and easy to understand as possible. Of course, unlike an attorney advising an individual client, we cannot cover every conceivable possibility.

COST/VALUE ANALYSIS

Whenever you shop for a product or service, you are faced with various levels of quality and price. In deciding what product or service to buy, you make a cost/value analysis on the basis of your willingness to pay and the quality you desire.

When buying a car, you decide whether you want transportation, comfort, status, or sex appeal. Accordingly, you decide among such choices as a Neon, a Lincoln, a Rolls Royce, or a Porsche. Before making a decision, you usually weigh the merits of each option against the cost.

When you get a headache, you can take a pain reliever (such as aspirin) or visit a medical specialist for a neurological examination. Given this choice, most people, of course, take a pain reliever, since it costs only pennies; whereas a medical examination costs hundreds of dollars and takes a lot of time. This is usually a logical choice because it is rare to need anything more than a pain reliever for a headache. But in some cases, a headache may indicate a brain tumor and failing to see a specialist right away can result in complications. Should everyone with a headache go to a specialist? Of course not, but people treating their own illnesses must realize that they are betting on the basis of their cost/value analysis of the situation. They are taking the most logical option.

The same cost/value analysis must be made when deciding to do one's own legal work. Many legal situations are very straight forward, requiring a simple form and no complicated analysis. Anyone with a little intelligence and a book of instructions can handle the matter without outside help.

But there is always the chance that complications are involved that only an attorney would notice. To simplify the law into a book like this, several legal cases often must be condensed into a single sentence or paragraph. Otherwise, the book would be several hundred pages long and too complicated for most people. However, this simplification necessarily leaves out many details and nuances that would apply to special or unusual situations. Also, there are many ways to interpret most legal questions. Your case may come before a judge who disagrees with the analysis of our authors.

Therefore, in deciding to use a self-help law book and to do your own legal work, you must realize that you are making a cost/value analysis. You have decided that the money you will save in doing it yourself outweighs the chance that your case will not turn out to your satisfaction. Most people handling their own simple legal matters never have a problem, but occasionally people find that it ended up costing them more to have an attorney straighten out the situation than it would have if they had hired an attorney in the beginning. Keep this in mind while handling your case, and be sure to consult an attorney if you feel you might need further guidance.

LOCAL RULES   The next thing to remember is that a book which covers the law for the entire nation, or even for an entire state, cannot possibly include every procedural difference of every jurisdiction. Whenever possible, we provide the exact form needed; however, in some areas, each county may require unique forms and procedures. In our state books, our forms usually cover the majority of counties in the state, or provide examples of the type of form which will be required. In our national books, our forms are sometimes even more general in nature but are designed to give a good idea of the type of form that will be needed in most locations. Nonetheless, keep in mind that your state or county may have a requirement, or use a form, that is not included in this book.

CHANGES IN   You should not necessarily expect to be able to get all of the informa-
THE LAW   tion and resources you need solely from within the pages of this book. This book will serve as your guide, giving you specific information whenever possible and helping you to find out what else you will need to know. This is just like if you decided to build your own backyard deck. You might purchase a book on how to build decks. However, such a book would not include the building codes and permit requirements of every city, town, county, and township in the nation; nor would it include the lumber, nails, saws, hammers, and other materials and tools you would need to actually build the deck. You would use the book as your guide, and then do some work and research involving such matters as whether you need a permit of some kind, what type and grade of wood is available in your area, whether to use hand tools or power tools, and how to use those tools.

Before using the forms in a book like this, you should check with your court clerk to see if there are any local rules of which you should be aware, or local forms you will need to use. Often, such forms will require the same information as the forms in the book but are merely laid out differently or use slightly different language. They will sometimes require additional information.

Besides being subject to local rules and practices, the law is subject to change at any time. The courts and the legislatures of all fifty states are constantly revising the laws. It is possible that while you are reading this book, some aspect of the law is being changed.

In most cases, the change will be of minimal significance. A form will be redesigned, additional information will be required, or a waiting period will be extended. As a result, you might need to revise a form, file an extra form, or wait out a longer time period; these types of changes will not usually affect the outcome of your case. On the other hand, sometimes a major part of the law is changed, the entire law in a particular area is rewritten, or a case that was the basis of a central legal point is overruled. In such instances, your entire ability to pursue your case may be impaired.

To help you with local requirements and changes in the law, be sure to read the section in chapter 1 on "Finding the Law: Legal Research."

Again, you should weigh the value of your case against the cost of an attorney and make a decision as to what you believe is in your best interest.

INTRODUCTION

The nonprofit organization is a particularly American institution. As early as the 1830s, de Toqueville remarked that Americans were "constantly forming associations." Today, the United States has the most advanced system of nonprofit organizations in the world. While other societies expect the government to provide for all of their citizens' needs, Americans rely on each other and are eager to volunteer when needed to improve society. This is a part of the independent spirit that has always influenced this country.

There are over a million nonprofit organizations in the country at this time which make up over twelve percent of the economy. They are estimated to control nearly two trillion dollars in assets. And as our society becomes wealthier in the new century, we can expect many more nonprofit organizations to be formed. The new millionaires and billionaires cannot possibly spend all their wealth on themselves or their families, so they will likely direct some of it into organizations which promote causes which they favor.

Whether you have enough money to fund a nonprofit organization yourself, or plan to rely on the generosity of others, the nonprofit corporation is the best vehicle for aiding a cause in which you believe. And whether you seek a cure for cancer or just closer ties among your ethnic group, the nonprofit corporation can help you claim all the benefits given to such organizations and establish something which can continue forever.

The benefits of nonprofit status are numerous. The best known of these is the tax-free status. But nonprofits also enjoy lower postage rates, discounts from some businesses, lower governmental fees, the ability to qualify for private and government grants and free air time or ads by some media outlets. Many nonprofits can attract funds from taxpayers because donations to them are deductible.

You can show that you have another American trait—the do-it-yourself entrepreneurial spirit—by using this book. Rather than hire a lawyer and pay "full freight," you can do a lot of the work yourself and save a lot of money to put toward your cause. However, you should realize that the law of nonprofit organizations is complicated. There are a lot of strict government rules which must be followed in order to qualify for all of the benefits. In some situations, you may need to pay for expert advice to be sure you have done everything right. The most complicated areas in the text will be noted and you will be advised when legal guidance may be necessary.

Fortunately, there are a lot of organizations whose purpose it is to help other nonprofits. Also, a lot of information is on the Internet. (Perhaps too much!) A recent search turned up over a million sites. But we have found some of the best sites and refer to them throughout the text.

Good luck with your new organization!

WHAT IS A NONPROFIT ORGANIZATION? 1

The basic definition of a nonprofit organization is that it is one which does not pass its income to its members or shareholders, but rather, it uses the income in the furtherance of a goal which benefits the community or some part of the community.

This doesn't mean that the operations of a nonprofit cannot be profitable. Many nonprofits make large profits on their operations, but those profits must not benefit private parties. They must be used to further the organization's stated goal. If a nonprofit disbands, no one except another qualified nonprofit organization (with as similar goals as possible) can take over its assets.

ADVANTAGES OF NONPROFIT STATUS

There are four main advantages of being a nonprofit organization rather than an ordinary business: the tax exemptions, the ability to receive tax-deductible donations, the ability to qualify for grants, and lower costs for such things as postage, advertising, and filing fees.

TAX EXEMPTION   For many nonprofits, the tax exemptions are the most important benefits. Several exemptions from taxes are available depending on the type of organization and the state in which it is located.

Income received by most nonprofits is not subject to income tax at either the state or federal level if you successfully apply for and are granted an exemption. In most states, you can get an exemption from paying sales and use taxes on items that the organization purchases. Also, many nonprofits do not have to pay property taxes on the real estate they own. Again, you must apply for, and be granted, the exemption.

DEDUCTIBILITY OF CONTRIBUTIONS

Perhaps more important than being tax exempt, contributions made by taxpayers to certain types of nonprofits are *deductible* on the taxpayer's income tax return. This is a big incentive to give and without this deduction, many nonprofits would not survive. The laws about soliciting donations are covered in chapter 6.

GRANTS

Being a nonprofit organization makes your group eligible for both private and government grants. There are many large foundations which are required by law to give away a percentage of their assets each year, but they can only do so to qualified nonprofit organizations. Applying for grants is discussed in chapter 6.

LOWER COSTS

The postal service offers special rates to nonprofit organizations, and these rates are much lower than the normal rates. Some newspapers, magazines, radio stations, and other media give discounted advertising rates to nonprofits. It is even possible in some cases for nonprofit organizations to get free advertising, also known as public service announcements.

TAX EXEMPT BONDS

Some types of nonprofit organizations are able to raise money by issuing tax-exempt bonds which are similar to municipal bonds. This is usually done by organizations like hospitals which need to finance multi-million dollar facilities.

DISADVANTAGES OF NONPROFIT STATUS

The benefits of nonprofit status would be useful to nearly all types of businesses and organizations, and many businesses could successfully operate as nonprofits. But there are disadvantages that go with them which make them unworkable to many types of organizations. In recent years, some for-profit businesses have complained that nonprofits were competing against them unfairly. So, the laws have been changed to make it more difficult for nonprofits to engage in activities which compete with for-profit businesses.

LOSS OF CONTROL
One of the most important things to know about a nonprofit organization is that it is not "owned" by its founders. Unlike a private business that can be sold after it has grown big and profitable, a nonprofit organization "belongs" to the public at large. If it dissolves, its assets must be given to another nonprofit organization with a purpose as close as possible to its purpose. If its assets are misapplied or used for private benefit by the officers, the state attorney general (or similar official) can seize them.

If you are planning to put a lot of money and years of your life into an organization, you should consider whether the advantages are worth the loss of control. But there are ways to set up a nonprofit to give yourself de facto control, and you are allowed to pay yourself a reasonable salary and set up a pension plan. The limits on these are discussed later in the book.

LIMITED PURPOSES
In order to be exempt under the tax laws, a nonprofit organization can only perform certain functions listed in those laws. If it goes outside those limits, it may have to pay taxes on some of its income, pay penalties, or lose its exemption entirely.

LIMITED LOBBYING
Most types of tax exempt nonprofit organizations are forbidden from contributing to political campaigns and may only do a limited amount of lobbying. This is discussed in more detail in chapter 5.

PUBLIC SCRUTINY
Another disadvantage is public scrutiny. Because a nonprofit organization is dedicated to the public, your finances are open to public inspection. This means that the public can obtain copies of your tax returns and find out your salaries and other expenditures.

LAWS THAT APPLY TO NONPROFIT ORGANIZATIONS

There are three main sets of laws which apply to nonprofit organizations. State corporation laws control the formation and operation of the organization. State charitable solicitation laws control the activities of the organization if it is soliciting donations from the public. Federal tax law governs what types of organizations can qualify as tax exempt, and what types of activities may be undertaken by tax exempt organizations.

STATE LAWS

State corporation law covers the formation of the nonprofit corporation. It sets the requirements for the articles of organization, the procedures for amendments, and the other structural and operational issues.

A summary of each state's laws is included in appendix B. You can use this summary to get an idea of how your organization can be formed and will be regulated. However, you should also obtain copies of the statutes themselves. In running your organization, you will want to be sure not to violate any of them.

State charitable solicitation laws regulate organizations which solicit money from the public and are designed to protect consumers from fraud. There have been numerous cases in which organizations claimed to be collecting money to fight cancer or feed the hungry but actually kept most of the money for themselves.

Not all states regulate charitable solicitation, and each of the states that do have different requirements. Whether a state has regulations, the exemption, and address to write to are in appendix B. More information on the requirements is in chapter 6.

FEDERAL TAX LAWS

Federal tax law is far more important than state law. The federal tax law controls what a nonprofit may or may not do if it wishes to take advantage of the tax exemptions.

State laws are usually very broad and allow nonprofits wide leeway in their purposes. Nearly any small group which doesn't intend to distribute its profit to its members could easily come under the nonprofit law of most states. However, the federal tax law applicable to nonprofits is very strict. It is also contradictory and confusing. This is because every few years Congress gets upset about some perceived abuse and tightens the laws. Consider the following:

☞ Because rich donors were setting up nonprofits to hire their family members and avoid estate taxes, a law was passed saying that nonprofits were forbidden to benefit private parties (the private inurement doctrine). But what about nonprofit social clubs whose sole purpose is to benefit their members? Well, they can only benefit their members and not serve the public.

☞ Because the government doesn't want to give tax benefits to groups that discriminate, nonprofits are forbidden from discriminating on the basis of race, religion, etc. But what about religious nonprofit organizations? Well, they can discriminate on the basis of religion if they have a good reason.

☞ To be sure the government doesn't subsidize groups that support those who hold office, nonprofits aren't allowed to contribute to political campaigns. However, they can set up political action committees (PACs), which are also nonprofit organizations but which have as their *sole purpose* contributing to political campaigns.

Every year the IRS issues new Revenue Rulings, the courts issue new opinions, and usually Congress tinkers with the law. How can you ever hope to comply with such a system? Keep in mind that the people enforcing the law are no more intelligent than you and in many cases they are as confused as you. A large percentage of the answers given on the IRS phone lines are wrong. *Money* magazine sends out sample income information to fifty accounting firms each year and every one of them comes up with a different tax amount, usually differing by thousands of dollars. There is no one alive who understands the entire tax code!

So here is your best strategy:

☞ Learn as much about the laws as you can and make a good faith effort to follow them carefully. If you are planning something that might be questionable, ask a tax specialist for an opinion.

☞ Keep good records.

☞ If your tax return or activities are questioned, make it clear that you are doing your best to comply and cooperate fully. (But get the best tax advice you can afford to be sure of your rights.)

OTHER
LAWS

Other than the specific laws for nonprofits, most laws that apply to other businesses also apply to nonprofits. In most states, for example, the general rules for business corporation procedure apply to nonprofit corporations. And federal election laws apply to nonprofit corporations as well as business corporations.

PERMITTED PURPOSES

A nonprofit organization may be formed for any legal purpose under most state laws, as long as it does not pass its profits on to its members, but in order to qualify for favorable tax treatment and gain other benefits, it must limit its purposes to those allowed in the Internal Revenue Code (IRC). The following are some of the most popular purposes which are allowed by the laws.

SECTION
501(C)(3)
ORGANIZATIONS

The best tax treatment is available to nonprofits which can qualify under section 501(c)(3) of the IRC. These organizations get both a tax exemption and the ability of their contributors to deduct contributions. Permitted purposes under this section include:

Religious. Religion is the oldest and broadest category of nonprofit. Because the First Amendment to the Constitution bars the government from making any law which prohibits the free exercise of religion, it is limited in how much it can regulate religious activities. However, to qualify for a tax exemption, some courts have required newly formed religious groups to be similar to traditional religions with such things as an established congregation, an organized ministry, regular services, education of the young, and a doctrinal code. This was done to keep people from setting up their own religions just for tax purposes.

Charitable. Under the tax law, the word "charitable" is broader than the normal definition of relieving poverty. Court decisions over the years have allowed all of the following types of activities to be undertaken by organizations which qualify for 501(c)(3) status.

☛ *Relief of poverty*. This can include any type of activity which gives aid to the poor such as soup kitchens or homeless shelters. But it must direct its benefit to the public at large, and not any particular person. For example, a group that formed to help a particular family that lost its home in a fire would not qualify for tax exempt status. It would need to have its purpose as helping all fire victims in a certain area to qualify.

☛ *Beautifying the community*. Groups which plant trees and clean up highways can qualify for charitable status. The limitation is that they must serve a broad community such as a city or town. If they only serve a limited number of people, such as a subdivision, they would not qualify for charitable status.

☛ *Lessening the burdens of government*. This category would be for groups that help existing government programs, such as improving parks, police facilities, or other government functions.

☛ *Promoting health*. Hospitals, blood banks, clinics, mental health organizations, and similar functions all qualify for charitable status as long as their profits do not go to private individuals.

☛ *Promoting social welfare*. This would include groups that support civil rights or promote community alliance, national defense, or similar causes.

☛ *Promoting environmental conservation*. This would include preserving national resources.

☞ *Promoting the arts.* This would cover groups that sponsor arts festivals, theatre groups, and concerts, as well as programs to encourage young people to develop their talents.

☞ *Promoting patriotism.* Groups that participate in patriotic displays and "inculcate patriotic emotions" are considered charitable for tax purposes.

☞ *Promoting amateur sports.* This would include little leagues and soccer clubs, but not any group which provides athletic facilities or equipment.

Scientific. Scientific research which is theoretical is clearly allowable for charitable nonprofit organizations, but research which is practical and has business applications is not. Testing products is not considered charitable (unless done for public safety) and doing work for one particular company is clearly not allowed.

Testing for public safety. Organizations like Underwriters Laboratories, which test the safety of products, are tax exempt.

Literary. Literary organizations are exempt if their work is not commercial, but rather, promotes the literacy of the community. For example, a publisher that sold books at normal prices would probably not qualify, but one which sought out unknown talented people and made their works available at a discount would.

Educational. Educational organizations can include libraries and museums as well as traditional schools, colleges, and universities. The important factor for the tax exemption is that the school be an objective place of learning rather than a promoter of a particular idea.

Preventing cruelty to children or animals. These organizations would include groups like the SPCA, orphanages, or any group that would aid children or animals as long as they are not limited to any particular child or animal.

There are two tests the IRS uses to determine if an organization qualifies under § 501(c)(3), the *organizational test* and the *operational test*.

Under the organizational test, the documentation which forms the organization must limit its purpose and activities to those which are allowable. For this reason, it is very important that the articles of incorporation and the bylaws are carefully drafted to pass IRS examination.

Under the operational test, the operations or activities must also comply with the law. It is not enough that the paperwork of the organization is correct, it must also conduct itself in conformance with those rules.

OTHER TYPES OF ORGANIZATIONS

If the purpose or activities of a nonprofit organization do not qualify it for an exemption under 501(c)(3), it still may claim an exemption under one of the other subsections of 501(c). The disadvantage is that under most of these subsections, the income is tax exempt, but contributions may not be deducted on donors tax returns.

The rationale for these other types of tax-exempt organizations is completely different from 501(c)(3) organizations. While the latter are exempt because they are perceived to be doing something beneficial to society, these others are not taxed because they are in effect just people pooling money to do something which would not be taxed if the money were not pooled.

For example, if a number of people use their money to lobby for better roads or to socialize every Sunday night, there is no tax involved, so if they put their money together in an organization to do the same thing, there is no reason they should have to pay an extra tax on that money.

The problem arises when these groups try to raise money from outside sources. If a social club charges its members $10 for dinner, but charges outside guests $20 for the same dinner, then someone (the members who pay less) are making a "profit" on the arrangement. This type of activity by a nonprofit organization is subject to tax.

Some organizations divide their operations into two or more nonprofit organizations. For example, a 501(c)(3) organization may have a subsidiary under another subsection to perform activities forbidden under its rules.

The following are some of the most common tax exempt organizations other than 501(c)(3)s:

Civic and social welfare associations. An organization can be formed under § 501(c)(4) to promote the common good and social welfare of a community. This is a type of organization you could use if you wanted to do something forbidden to 501(c)(3) organizations, such as lobby for better roads or school. Because contributions to these organizations are not deductible, you should try to fit your purpose into a 501(c)(3) by concentrating on allowable purposes, and only choose this form if that is impossible.

Employee associations. Also under § 501(c)(4), an association of employees of one employer can be formed if their net earnings are devoted exclusively to charitable, educational, or recreational purposes.

Labor organizations. A labor or agricultural worker organization can be formed under § 501(c)(5) if their goal is better conditions or improving production or efficiency.

Trade associations. Groups which promote the common interest of a business community or a line of businesses, such as a chamber of commerce or board of real estate are exempt under § 501(c)(6). However, a group may not carry on business itself, it may only promote the interests of all businesses in the same field.

It is important that a trade association be involved with only one trade. If it is a group of people from different trades who meet to network, it will not qualify under 501(c)(6), though it may be able to qualify as a social club or other type of exempt organization. It must allow competitors in the same field to be members; it cannot support only one faction of an industry.

Social clubs. A club which is formed solely for pleasure and recreational purposes is exempt under § 501(c)(7) if most of its income is from member dues and only an insubstantial amount is raised from the public.

With the strict rules that a nonprofit organization cannot give any benefits to its members, it seems anomalous that a group whose sole purpose is to benefit its members could qualify. But as explained above, there is no reason to tax groups which merely pool their money to do something which would not be taxed if paid for separately.

In order to qualify as a tax exempt social club, an organization must have a membership which commingles and has shared interests. Groups which have been allowed are fraternities and sororities, lunch and dinner clubs, golf and tennis clubs, gem collectors, large families, and political clubs to name a few. One organization which was disallowed an exemption was an auto club because the IRS found that the interests of the members were too different.

Cemeteries. If a cemetery is set up, not to make a profit but to provide plots exclusively for its members, it can be tax exempt under § 501(c)(13).

Veterans' organizations. If seventy-five percent of the members of a veterans' organization are past or present members of the armed forces and most of the rest are relatives of veterans, it can qualify as tax exempt under § 501(c)(19).

PROHIBITED PRACTICES

There are certain things which nonprofit organizations are prohibited from doing. Violation of those rules can cause loss of tax-exempt status or even penalties and fines.

Many of these rules were enacted when nonprofit organizations were seen to be abusing their status. When one nonprofit opposed the re-election of a certain United States Senator, he got a law passed to prohibit them from political activities. When some rich families began using nonprofit organizations to employ their family members, laws were passed to prohibit such arrangements. Every few years, someone does an exposé of abuses at nonprofits and new laws are proposed to control them. As a nonprofit organization, your group will want to keep abreast of proposals for changes in the law.

There are big differences in what charitable [§ 501(c)(3)] groups can do (those that can collect tax deductible contributions) and what other nonprofits can do. The limits are much more strict for charitable groups because the deductibility of their income is considered a government subsidy which should go to the good of the community rather than a few individuals.

The following are the major prohibitions for nonprofit organizations.

NO SPECIFIC BENEFIT

For nonprofit organizations to qualify as charitable, the focus of their mission must be the community at large, not any individual or small group of individuals. For example, you can get an exemption for a group that wants to aid tornado victims, but not for a group formed to help one specific victim. Similarly, you can get an exemption to clean up an entire community, but not just one subdivision.

Groups that do benefit limited numbers of people, such as social clubs, trade groups, and homeowners associations, can be nonprofit and tax exempt, but the members' dues are not deductible and their outside income must be limited.

NO PRIVATE INUREMENT

Similar to the requirement that the purpose of the nonprofit be to aid the community, the *private inurement doctrine* mandates that private parties not get undue profits from a nonprofit organization.

This means that the organizer and directors cannot get inflated salaries or other unusual financial arrangements. Business dealings between a nonprofit and persons related to it are put under careful scrutiny and can result in penalties or loss of tax exemption if found to be unreasonable.

Business dealings are allowed between nonprofits and their members and directors, but they should be at commercially reasonable terms. For example, if an organization rents an office from one if its directors, the rent should be documented as fair and reasonable. If it is inflated, the organization's tax status is in jeopardy.

In the real world, nonprofits get away with a lot more than the law books would have you believe. Exposés by such publications as *U.S. News & World Report* and *The Philadelphia Inquirer* uncovered nonprofit officers making hundreds of thousands, even millions, of dollars in salaries, guaranteed loans, and numerous other alleged abuses.

LIMITED
LOBBYING

Because of perceived abuses, Congress has put strict restraints on the type of lobbying that can be done by charitable organizations. However, no such limits apply to nonprofit organizations which are not charitable.

Charitable nonprofits. Charitable nonprofit organizations (those whose contributions are deductible) are prohibited from contributing to political campaigns and their lobbying cannot be *substantial.* Private foundations cannot lobby at all, and other charitable organizations must stick to certain limits. The exact limits are determined by applying either the *expenditure test* or the *substantial part test.* This is explained in more detail in chapter 5.

Other nonprofits. Nonprofits that are not charitable (social welfare, trade associations, social clubs, labor unions) are free to lobby as long as the lobbying is related to their specific organizational goal (exempt function). One limitation is that if the dues of members are used for lobbying, then that amount may not be deducted as a business expense (or any other way) by the members.

Political organizations. Organizations which are formed to support particular political candidates can be nonprofits and give unlimited amounts to campaigns, but they are not supposed to lobby to influence legislation because it is not part of their exempt function, namely supporting particular candidates.

LIMITED
COMMERCIAL
ACTIVITIES

Because of complaints by businesses that they cannot compete with tax exempt organizations that are in the same business, nonprofit organizations are limited in the types of commercial activities in which they can engage. If a nonprofit does engage in a business venture that is unrelated to its purpose, the profits from that venture are taxable. But if a nontaxable organization has too much taxable income, it may lose its status as tax exempt. For this reason, successful nonprofit groups, such as the National Geographic Society, have had to spin off operations which became too profitable.

Fortunately, there are some loopholes which nonprofits can use to make money and still avoid paying tax. These include selling donated items, performing services provided by volunteers, and giving away small items. For more details see chapter 5.

WHAT TYPE OF NONPROFIT IS BEST? 2

Before forming a nonprofit organization, you should understand the types of structures which are available so that you can choose the one which will provide the most benefits to the type of organization you are planning.

ASSOCIATION, TRUST, OR CORPORATION

A nonprofit organization can organize itself in any of three ways: as an unincorporated association, a trust, or a corporation. For most groups, a corporation offers the most advantages, but in certain situations, the others may work better.

ASSOCIATION   Any type of informal group of people who get together for a common purpose can be considered an unincorporated association. Technically, a group of people which act as a group, such as a bridge club, PTA, or ski club, is an unincorporated association. Such a group has some legal rights as such, like the right to open a bank account. However, this structure has some legal liabilities. For example, if the members of a ski club are driving together and get into an accident because of the negligence of the member driving, it is possible that all members of the club could be liable to the person injured, whether or not that person is a club member. For this reason, groups that are involved in risky activities are advised to incorporate. Small groups of friends who do things together usually do not have to worry. Their auto and homeowners' insurance will cover most possible risks. But if the club expands beyond a small group of friends, starts generating income, or wishes to apply for grants or deductible donations, it should incorporate for the advantages listed below.

TRUST A few types of nonprofit organizations are more often formed as trusts. For example, charitable gifts made in wills are often set up as charitable trusts. Also, political committees are set up as trusts because federal election laws prohibit corporations from giving money to political campaigns. Multi-employer pension plans must be set up as trusts and many other pension plans are as well.

However, for most groups that have members this is not a good entity. One problem is that the trustees are not protected against liability and, in fact, may have a greater exposure to liability because trustees are held to a higher, *fiduciary* standard. This means that they must be extremely careful in their dealings or they can be personally liable for their mistakes.

CORPORATION The corporation is the most common, and best, form for a nonprofit organization. Here are some of the benefits:

Protection from liability. The officers, directors, and members of a nonprofit corporation are protected, in most cases, from liability for the debts and obligations of the corporation. If the corporation incurs debts or if someone is injured by a member of the corporation, the others in the organization normally would not be personally liable. There are exceptions to this, however. If the officers or members personally guarantee the debt, or if they cause the injury, they will be liable.

Eligibility for grants. Many government and private programs can only make their grants to organizations which are incorporated.

Procedural rules. When an organization incorporates, it is then governed by state incorporation law. This law usually answers all of the issues that come up in such an organization, such as how many directors there must be, what is a valid quorum, and what are the rights of members. If the organization is unincorporated, it must make up its own procedures for all of these types of contingencies.

There is a price to pay for these benefits, but it is well worth it. The price is that the organization must register with a state and must make periodic filings and disclosures. There are also filing fees, but these are usually small. If professionals are retained to prepare these documents, the cost may be high, but this is not necessary for small groups whose affairs are not complicated.

DOMESTIC OR FOREIGN

The first decision which must be made when forming a nonprofit corporation is whether it will be *domestic* (formed in the state in which it is operating) or *foreign* (formed in another state). In nearly all cases, it is best to use a domestic corporation because the paperwork for registering a foreign corporation in the state in which you are operating is about the same as forming a corporation there. Also, there is an extra registration fee and you must hire a registered agent in the state in which the foreign corporation is formed.

REASONS FOR
INCORPORATING
OUT-OF-STATE

There are two good reasons to use a foreign nonprofit corporation. One is if you wish to have less than three directors and your state requires three. Many nonprofits have more than three directors because this broadens support and looks better to grant makers and the IRS. But some people who intend to put a lot of their time and money into a new organization are not willing to share the power to make decisions for it. It may be possible to get friends or relatives to be the additional directors, but if this is not convenient for you, you could incorporate in a state that allows a single director.

The following states allow a single director in a nonprofit corporation:

California   New Hampshire (requires 5 incorporators)
Colorado   Oklahoma

Delaware	Oregon
Idaho	Pennsylvania
Iowa	South Carolina (requires 2 incorporators)
Kansas	Virginia
Michigan	Washington
Mississippi	West Virginia

In New Hampshire and South Carolina, although only one person need be a director, five and two persons, respectively, need to sign the incorporation papers to get the organization started.

A second reason to use another state is if you wish to have a *stock-based* nonprofit corporation, and your state does not allow it. A stock-based nonprofit corporation is one which is controlled by its stockholders. This is one way to keep control of the organization in a limited number of persons. Of course, the stockholders cannot receive any dividends or profits of the organization.

Most states do not allow nonprofits to be set up as stock based so to use one you would need to set up the organization in a state which does. First check with your state to see if a stock-based nonprofit is allowed to qualify to do business there because in some states, they cannot.

MEMBERSHIP OR NONMEMBERSHIP

A nonprofit corporation must decide whether to have members and if it does have members, whether there will be different classes of members, such as voting and non-voting.

Allowing people to become members of a nonprofit organization may seem like a good way to get their support but because formal members of nonprofits are granted legal rights to control it, many organizations decide against formal membership, at least in the beginning. In most states, formal members have a right to vote on major decisions and to choose directors or officers. This can be both time-consuming and costly and opens the risk that a splinter group may take over the organization. Consider, for example, if a group of concerned citizens organizes a group to fight the pollution of a chemical plant. If the plant asks all its employees to join the organization, they could become a majority and vote to disband it.

One way to keep control even with a membership corporation is to provide that the officers and directors are elected from a slate chosen by a nominating committee. This committee can be composed of the founding members and those they approve.

However, the easiest way to keep control of a nonprofit corporation is to set it up as a nonmembership organization. The bylaws included in this book in appendix C are for a nonmembership corporation. If you wish to have a membership organization, you can use the Amendment to Bylaws or rewrite them including those sections.

To give people an incentive to support an organization, they can be given an informal membership or be listed as "benefactors," "contributors," "associates," or a similar title. This would give them the feeling of being part of the organization without the power to control its affairs.

CHARITABLE OR NONCHARITABLE

The law of nonprofit organizations can be confusing because there are two meanings for the word *charitable*. One is a charity which, for example, aids the poor. The other is the broader IRS definition which includes all organizations which can accept tax-deductible contributions. These include educational, religious, scientific, patriotic, and many other types of organizations which are allowed under section 501(c)(3) of the Internal Revenue Code.

If at all possible, you should form your organization to comply with this section and therefore become a *charitable organization*. To do so, you must draft your statement of purpose to fit into the allowable purposes under the law. This is explained in more detail in chapter 4.

If you cannot possibly fit your planned activities into a 501(c)(3) organization (such as if you plan to do substantial lobbying for new laws or contribute to political campaigns), you can form a *noncharitable* nonprofit organization under one of the other exemptions. These include:

- ☞ Business leagues (trade associations) under § 501(c)(6)
- ☞ Chambers of commerce under § 501(c)(6)
- ☞ Civic leagues under § 501(c)(4)
- ☞ Employee associations under § 501(c)(4), (9), or (17)
- ☞ Labor organizations under § 501(c)(5)
- ☞ Lodges under § 501(c)(10)
- ☞ Recreational clubs under § 501(c)(7)
- ☞ Social clubs under § 501(c)(7)
- ☞ Social welfare organizations under § 501(c)(4)
- ☞ Veterans organizations under § 501(c)(19)

Under these sections, you can be an organization exempt from paying income taxes, but contributions given to you will not be tax deductible to the contributors as charitable contributions. They might be tax deductible for another reason. For example, dues to a trade association are usually tax deductible to businesses in the same trade.

PUBLIC CHARITY OR PRIVATE FOUNDATION

If you are able to be a charitable organization under § 501(c)(3), the next determination will be whether your organization is a *public charity* or a *private foundation*. But there really is no choice because every nonprofit should endeavor to avoid private foundation status. This status can result in some very difficult rules.

PUBLIC
CHARITY

All new charitable organizations are presumed to be private foundations unless they can pass certain tests and become public charities. There are three ways to become classified as a public charity: automatic qualification, passing the public support test, or passing the facts and circumstances test. These are spelled out in detail in IRS Publication 557 and are summarized below.

Automatic qualification. A charity automatically qualifies as public if it is one of the following types of organizations:

☛ A church

☛ A school with formal instruction and a regularly enrolled student body

☛ A hospital

☛ A medical research facility

☛ A public safety organization

☛ An organization that supports one of the above

Public support test. If a charity does not qualify automatically for public charity status, it can qualify if it received broad public support. For this, the IRS requires an organization to receive at least one-third of its total financial support from public support sources.

Facts and circumstances test. If a charity cannot pass the public support test, there is yet a third way to qualify. First, it must receive at least ten percent of its funding as public support. Next, it must carry on *bona fide programs* to attract public support on a continual basis. Finally, the IRS will look at the following five factors:

☛ The percentage of public support

☛ The sources of the support

☛ The makeup of the governing body

☛ The benefits available to the public from the organization

☛ The makeup of the membership and audience of the organization

An organization does not have to satisfy all five factors, but they will be weighed depending on the nature of the organization.

PRIVATE
FOUNDATIONS

If a nonprofit organization cannot qualify for public charity status through any of the above tests, it will be classified as a private foundation. As a private foundation, it must comply with the following rules under the IRC:

☞ Distribute its income each year so as not to be subject to § 4942 tax

☞ Avoid any self-dealing as defined in § 4941(d)

☞ Not retain business holdings as defined in § 4943(c)

☞ Not make any investments which are taxable under § 4944

☞ Not make any expenditures as defined in § 4945(d)

It must also pay an excise tax on its investment income.

Donors who give to a private foundation can only take a deduction of up to thirty percent of their adjusted gross income; whereas for a public charity, they can deduct up to fifty percent.

Private operating foundations. If they can become classified as *private operating foundations*, private foundations can qualify for donors deducting fifty percent of their contributions, and they can be relieved of the requirement to distribute funds received from private foundations within one year. To qualify, they must meet the *asset test*, the *support test*, or the *endowment test* and distribute eighty-five percent of their income each year. For more information, see IRS Publication 557.

Exempt operating foundations. A third possibility is for a private foundation is to qualify as an *exempt operating foundation*. As an exempt operating foundation, an organization does not have to pay the excise tax on net investment income. A private operating foundation can qualify as exempt if it has been publicly supported for at least ten years, has a governing body which broadly represents the public, and if no officers and no more than twenty-five percent of the governing board are *disqualified individuals* (major donors or their family members). See IRS Publication 557 for more details.

START-UP PROCEDURES 3

SEND FOR FORMS AND INSTRUCTIONS

The first thing to do in forming your nonprofit corporation is to send for forms and instructions from your state's corporate registration division (usually the secretary of state), the state department of revenue, the office that regulates charitable solicitations, and from the Internal Revenue Service. These usually take a week or two to arrive so you can be working on the following sections while waiting for them.

STATE FORMS AND INSTRUCTIONS

What you need to ask for from the secretary of state is "any and all materials and forms available for forming a nonprofit corporation." Some states just give you a single page of obscure instructions while others give a large packet of forms, statutes, contact numbers, and other useful information. A letter which you can mail in is included in appendix C. You may get much faster service by phoning or using the state's website.

The address, phone number, and website for your state is on that state's page in appendix B. In some cases the entire information packet may be downloadable from their website, which may be your fastest way if you have computer access. If you plan to start a corporation in a state other than the one in which you are operating, you will need the information from both states.

You will need to obtain information and forms for obtaining an exemption from state taxes from your state department of revenue. The addresses, phone numbers, and websites are in appendix B and a form request letter is in appendix C. For some states, you may be able to download the material from the department of revenue website. The state tax exemptions are explained in more detail in chapter 4.

If you plan to do charitable solicitation, in most states you will need to obtain information on any registration requirements from the state attorney general's office (in a few states it is a different office). The address, phone number, and basic requirements are listed in appendix B. More details on charitable solicitation laws are included in chapter 6.

IRS FORMS AND INSTRUCTIONS

For IRS forms the fastest way to get them is to download them from the Internet at http://www.irs.ustreas.gov. However, because they are large booklets, it will tie up your line for a long time unless you have a fast connection. Another way to obtain them is to call the IRS forms office at 1-800-829-1040. (If this doesn't work in your area, check the federal government pages of your telephone book). What you will need is:

- Publication 557 Tax Exempt Status for Your Organization
- Package 1023 Application for Recognition of Exemption under § 501(c)(3)
- Package 1024 Application for Recognition of Exemption under sections other than § 501(c)(3)
- Publication 526 Charitable Contributions
- Publication 561 Determining the Value of Donated Property
- Publication 598 Tax on Unrelated Business Income

DEFINE YOUR PURPOSE

Before forming your nonprofit organization, you should have a clear picture of your purpose and goals. You should then review the allowable purposes under the Internal Revenue Code and decide what type of organization you can be.

You will want to fit your purpose into the requirements for a § 501(c)(3) organization, if at all possible, so that people who contribute money to you can deduct it on their taxes.

If your activities can fit into more than one area, you should stress the one that is allowable under § 501(c)(3). For example, if you are starting an organization because you are concerned about pesticides causing cancer, you should not focus on the fact that you may want to lobby for laws against pesticides that cause cancer. If your primary function is to research pesticides or to educate the public as to which ones may be harmful, you could qualify as a 501(c)(3) organization which does scientific research or public education. If you later wanted to lobby, you could do some within your organization, or you could form a separate organization to conduct substantial lobbying.

If the goal that you list on your application is one which the IRS feels can only be achieved by legislation, they will deny your exemption as a 501(c)(3) organization. In such a case, you will either have form a non-charitable organization or else redefine your goal. For example, a goal such as "abolishing nuclear weapons" would appear to be one which required legislation. However, if "educating the public on the dangers of nuclear proliferation" was your goal, then, depending on the programs you planned, you would have a better chance to qualify as charitable.

Review the IRS materials carefully and be sure that your purpose fits into one of the exempt categories. If you find this difficult, or feel you may not be successful, you may want to consult with an attorney specializing in nonprofit organizations. Since this is one of the most important applications your organization will file, it will be worth the investment to get it right.

CHOOSING AND SEARCHING YOUR NAME

While the activities and accomplishments of your organization will build up a reputation for its name, having a good name to begin with is a good way to appear more trustworthy. Also, the wrong kind of name (sounding like a commercial business) may raise questions with the IRS.

CHOOSING
A NAME

In choosing a name, you should use the following guidelines:

Use the right suffix. Some states require that certain words or suffixes be a part of the name of a company, such as "inc." or "assn." On the state sheets in appendix B and on the materials from your state, you will find the rules that apply to the corporation's name.

Don't use forbidden words. Certain words, such as "olympic" or "trust" are not allowed to be used as part of an organization's name under many states' laws. Most of these rules will be found either on the state sheets in appendix B or on the materials from your state.

Don't be too similar. While there might seem to be some advantage to having your name sound like a similar group, such as the American Cancer Society or the American Red Cross, this would leave you open to a lawsuit by the other organization and possibly legal action by your state attorney general. You can use words such as cancer, heart, or diabetes if it relates to your organization's purpose, but do not intentionally make your name sound like another group's name.

Be sure it's not confusing. Many words in the English language are spelled differently from how they sound. Be sure that the name you choose is easy to spell so that people can locate your phone number or web address easily. Someone once published a list of all the remaining English words which had not yet been registered with ".com" and most of them were hard to spell or had confusing homonyms.

SEARCHING
A NAME

Once you have chosen the perfect name, you need to be sure that no one else has established legal rights to it. Many business have been forced to stop using their name after spending thousands of dollars in promotions.

Legal rights can be established by registering a name as a trademark or by merely using the name. Consequently, you can't be sure no one has rights to a name just by checking registered names. You need to check to see if anyone is using the name who has not yet registered it.

The following are places you should check:

Federal trademarks. First, you should check to see if anyone has registered the name as a federal trademark. This can be done on the Internet at http://www.uspto.gov/tmdb/index.html. If you do not have access to the Internet at home, you can use a computer in many libraries. If you are not familiar with how to access the Internet, a librarian may be able to perform the search for you for a small fee.

Yellow pages. You should search the yellow page listings next. This can also be done online. Most sites check one state at a time, but the following site can check all states: http://www.switchboard.com. Since search engines are not always one hundred percent accurate, you should search on at least a few other sites for the state in which you will operate.

Web addresses. If you have any expectation of having a website some day, you should check to see if the web address (uniform resource locator, or URL) is available. This can be done at http://www.whois.com. As a nonprofit organization, you will be able to use the designation ".org" (rather than ".com" or ".net"), but if you have a clever name you wish to use with ".com" you can use that. If a clever name you want is already taken in ".org" ".com" and ".net," it may be available in the new designations ".cc" and ".to." However, because you would be similar to an existing group, you run the risk of getting sued and would be better off with a unique name.

Search services. If you are unable to get access to the Internet in any way, or if you would rather have someone else do the search, you can hire a professional search firm. In addition to a trademark search, they can check other records around the country and give you a more accurate answer as to whether the name is being used anywhere. The cost can range from about $100 to over $800 depending on how thorough the search is and who is doing it. The following are a few firms that do searches. You can call or write to them for a quote.

Government Liaison Services, Inc.
3030 Clarendon Blvd., Suite 209
P. O. Box 10648
Arlington, VA 22210
(800) 642-6564; (703) 524-8200

Thomson & Thomson
500 Victory Road
North Quincy, MA 02171-1545
(800) 692-8833

XL Corporate Service
62 White Street
New York, NY 10013
(800) 221-2972

Secretary of state. Finally, you should check with the secretary of state in the state in which you will register your corporation to see if the name is available. In some states, this can be done over the phone or on the Internet; in others, you must send a written inquiry.

REGISTERING THE NAME

After you have chosen the right name for your new company and made sure that it is still available and does not conflict with another name, you should register it before someone else does. You are allowed to reserve a name for a small fee in most states. However, it is usually better to just send in your articles of incorporation as soon as you decide upon a name.

By forming your corporation, you have insured that no other person can register a company with the same name in your state. Nonetheless, this does not stop someone from registering the name with another state or from getting a federal trademark for it.

TRADEMARKS

A federal trademark gives the owner the right to use the name anywhere in the United States and to stop most others from using it. But it does not cut off the rights of those who have used the name previously. For example, suppose you form an Italian-American social club named Vesuvius Club, do a search, find no one using it, and register the name as a trademark. If you later learn that there is a group which has been using the name Vesuvius Club in San Francisco before you started, but they don't have a trademark or telephone listing, you cannot stop them from using it in their area. Because of your federal trademark, you can stop any new clubs from using the name, but not those who used it before you began.

With the Internet reaching into every corner of the world, there is an issue of Internet businesses infringing on the rights of small operators in remote locations. If you plan an operation with a significant web presence, you may be sued by some small operator somewhere who has used the name before you. If you register a federal trademark and he hasn't, it would work in your favor, but there is now the open legal question of how thorough a business needs to be when doing a search.

One good way to see if anyone is using a name is to just do web searches on the major search engines (Yahoo, Excite, Altavista, Lycos) and see if your name is being used anywhere by anyone. If not, you are in good shape. If so, you need to determine if the other use conflicts with your intended use.

Before attempting to register your name, you should know the following basics of federal trademarks.

☞ A *trademark* is technically the name of a mark applied to goods while a *service mark* is a mark used on services. A nonprofit organization will usually provide services, so it will likely be registering a service mark.

☞ Trademarks and service marks are registered according to classes of goods or services. If you plan to use your mark in more than one class, you will need to register (and pay a filing fee of $325) for each class.

☞ Your trademark will not be granted until you have actually used the mark. You can file an application indicating your intent to use a mark, but you must actually use it before registration is accomplished.

☛ In order to qualify for federal registration, you must use your mark "in commerce," which means in a transaction between people in different states or with a foreign country. The use must be in good faith, meaning that you can't just mail a copy to a relative.

☛ You can register your trademark with each state. This is not necessary if you plan to get a federal trademark immediately; but if you plan to limit your business to one state or don't plan to expand out of state for a number of years, state registration is faster and cheaper than federal.

The entire procedure for registering a federal trademark is beyond the scope of this book, but you can get more information from the USPTO website (http://www.uspto.gov) or you can find all the forms and instructions in the book *How to Register Your Own Trademark* published by Sourcebooks.

ARTICLES OF INCORPORATION

To create a nonprofit corporation, a document must be filed with the state agency which keeps corporate records which is usually the Secretary of State. In most states, this document is called the *articles of incorporation*; however, in some states, it may be called the certificate of incorporation, articles of association, or charter. For simplicity, this document is referred to as the articles of incorporation throughout this book.

Most states provide a blank form for the articles of incorporation, and the IRS provides a sample of what they look for as articles of incorporation. Unfortunately, these two forms are in no way similar! What you will need to do in order to have articles which are acceptable to both your state and the IRS is to combine the requirements of both. This can be done in a few ways:

☛ We have included a generic articles of incorporation form with this book (form 4 in appendix C). This contains the IRS requirements for § 501(c)(3) organizations and the basic requirements of most states. You should check your state material to see if there are any new or additional requirements and, if so, add these to article 11 of our generic articles.

☛ Also included in this book is an addendum to articles of incorporation form (form 5 in appendix C) which includes the IRS requirements for § 501(c)(3) organizations. You can use this form as an addendum to your state's form. Of course this won't work for the states which do not provide blank articles of incorporation forms.

☛ You can take the requirements from your state's form and the IRS requirements from the addendum and retype them into a neat new articles of incorporation document.

If you are forming an organization which is exempt under a section other than § 501(c)(3) [e.g. social welfare organizations under § 501(c)(4) or social clubs under § 501(c)(7)], you will need to use the third option above and retype the material applicable to your type of organization. Some organizations have special requirements, for example, social clubs must be nondiscriminatory. For more information, see IRS Publication 557.

If you are forming a private foundation (even though, as explained in chapter 2, you should avoid a private foundation at all cost), you should obtain IRS Publication 578.

The following is a discussion of the articles included in the articles of incorporation form in this book. These articles are the common ones on most states' forms.

Article 1: Name of the corporation. Some states require nonprofit corporations to include a suffix like "Inc." or "Association" at the end of their name, but others do not. Check the state pages in appendix B for your state's requirements.

Article 2: Address of the corporation. The street address of the principal office and, if different, the mailing address of the corporation should be provided.

Article 3: Purpose. The first sentence is the required language to qualify for § 501(c)(3) status. After this, you must add the *specific* purpose of your organization. It is important to word this correctly or your exempt status may be denied by the IRS. Refer to IRS Publication 557 for guidance. If you have trouble drafting your purpose, you should consider consulting with a specialist in nonprofit law.

Article 4: Directors. Include the number of directors (most states require three but some allow just one) and their names and addresses.

Article 5: Private inurement and lobbying. This is the language required by the IRS to prevent the corporation from using its assets for private inurement or from lobbying the government.

Article 6: Dissolution. This is the requirement by the IRS that if the corporation dissolves the assets will go to another qualifying organization.

Article 7: The name of the registered agent and the address of the registered office along with the agent's acceptance. Each corporation must have a registered agent (in some states called a statutory agent) and a registered office. The registered office can be the business office of the corporation if the registered agent works out of that office. It can be the office of another individual who is the registered agent (such as the corporation's attorney) or it may be a professional registered agent's office. In some states, it may not be a residence unless that address is also a business office of the corporation. Penalty for failure to comply can be the inability to maintain a lawsuit and possibly a fine.

Article 8: Members. In this section check the box to designate whether or not the corporation will have members.

Article 9: Duration. In nearly all cases, you will want the duration of the corporation to be perpetual rather than for a set number of years.

Article 10: Name and address of the incorporator of the corporation. In some states, this may be any person, even if that person has no future interest in the corporation. There are companies in state capitols which will, on a moment's notice, have someone run over to the Secretary of

State to file corporate articles which are later assigned to the real parties in interest. It is possible in some states to file corporate papers by fax and to use a credit card for payment.

Article 11: Additional requirements. Review the state pages in appendix B and the materials from your state (or the state statute) to determine if any other matters are required to be included in the articles. If so, include them here. If more than one matter needs to be included, you can designate them Article 12, Article 13, etc.

EXECUTION

In most states, the Articles of Incorporation must be signed and dated by the incorporator in black ink. Typically, the registered agent must sign a statement accepting his duties as such. This is sometimes done as a separate form or sometimes on the same form as the articles.

FILING

The Articles of Incorporation must be filed with the Secretary of State by sending them to the address listed in appendix B along with the filing fees. A duplicate copy must be included in most states. The fees as available at time of publication are listed in Appendix B as well. If you wish to receive a certified copy of the articles, which you will need for the nonprofit mailing permit, the cost is additional.

The return time for the articles is usually a week or two in most states. If there is a need to have them back quickly, you might be able to send them and have them returned by a courier such as Federal Express, Airborne Express or UPS with prepaid return. Call your secretary of state for details.

BYLAWS

Every corporation must have bylaws. For a nonprofit corporation they are especially important and must be submitted to the IRS when applying for the tax exemption. This is the document which usually spells out in detail the corporations purpose, its operating rules, and operational structure.

A generic set of bylaws is included in this book in appendix C. You should read through this carefully and be sure that everything in it will apply to your organization and that there is no conflict with your state laws. If you wish to make any major changes to them (such as powers, voting, quorum), you should first check your state statutes to be sure that your provisions do not violate any section of the law.

As discussed in chapter 2, it is not advisable to have formal members, but if you do decide to have members, you will need to add membership provisions to your bylaws. These are included in the Addendum to Bylaws. Be sure to check the correct box in Article II in the bylaws if you use this.

TAXPAYER IDENTIFICATION NUMBER

Prior to opening a bank account, the corporation must obtain a taxpayer identification number (formally known as an Employer Identification Number or EIN) which is the corporate equivalent of a social security number. You will need this number even if you do not expect to hire employees.

The number is obtained by filing Form SS-4 which is included in this book in appendix D. This usually takes two or three weeks, so it should be filed early. Send the form to the Internal Revenue Service Center listed in the instructions.

If you need the identification number quickly you can obtain it by calling the IRS phone number included in the instructions. Be sure to have your SS-4 form complete before calling and have it in front of you.

When you apply for this number, you will probably be put on the mailing list for other corporate tax forms. If you do not receive these, you should call your local IRS office and request the forms for new businesses. These include Circular E explaining the taxes due, the W-4 forms for each employee, the tax deposit coupons, and the Form 941 quarterly return for withholding.

CORPORATE SUPPLIES

A corporation needs to keep a permanent record of its legal affairs. This includes the original state letter approving your organization, minutes of all meetings, lists of members, fictitious names registered, and any other legal matters. The records are usually kept in a ring binder. Any ring binder will do, but it is possible to purchase a specially prepared "corporate kit" which has the name of the corporation printed on it and usually contains forms such as minutes and bylaws. Most of these items are included with this book, so purchasing such a kit is unnecessary unless you want to have a fancy leather binder.

Some sources for corporate kits are:

Ace Industries, Inc.
54 NW 11th St.
Miami, FL 33136-9978
(305) 358-2571
(800) 433-2571

Midstate Legal Supply Co., Inc.
P. O. Box 2122
Orlando, FL 32802
(407) 299-8220
(800) 327-9220

Corpex
1440 5th Ave.
Bayshore, NY 11106
(800) 221-8181

CORPORATE SEAL One thing that is not included with this book is a corporate seal. This must be specially made for each corporation. Most corporations use a metal seal like a notary's seal to emboss the paper. This can be ordered from an office supply company. Some states now allow rubber stamps for corporate seals. These are cheaper, lighter, and easier to read. Rubber stamp seals can also be ordered from office supply stores, printers, and specialized rubber stamp companies. The corporate seal should contain the full, exact name of the corporation, the word "SEAL," and the year of incorporation.

ORGANIZATIONAL MEETING

The real birth of the corporation takes place at the initial meeting of the incorporators and the initial board of directors. The officers and board of directors are elected at this meeting. Other business may also take place, such as adopting employee benefit plans.

Usually, minutes and tax and other forms are prepared before the organizational meeting and used as a script for the meeting. They are read and voted on during the meeting and signed at the end of the meeting.

Those items in the following agenda designated with an asterisk (*) are forms found in appendix C of this book. These forms may be cut out of the book, photocopied, or rewritten as necessary to fit your situation.

The agenda for the initial meeting is usually as follows:

1. Signing the Waiver of Notice of the Meeting*

2. Noting Persons Present

3. Presentation and Acceptance of Articles of Incorporation* (the copy returned by the Secretary of State)

4. Election of Directors

5. Adoption of Bylaws*

6. Election of Officers

7. Presentation and Acceptance of Corporate Seal

8. Adoption of Banking Resolution*

9. Adoption of Resolution to Pay Expenses*

10. Adoption of any tax resolutions

11. Adjournment

Minute Book

After the organizational meeting, you should set up your minute book. As noted previously, this can be a fancy leather book or a simple ring binder. The minute book usually contains the following:

1. Title page ("Corporate Records of _____")
2. Table of contents
3. The letter from the Secretary of State acknowledging receipt and filing of the Articles of Incorporation
4. Copy of the Articles of Incorporation
5. Copy of any fictitious name registration
6. Copy of any trademark registration
7. Waiver of Notice of Organizational Meeting
8. Minutes of Organizational Meeting
9. Bylaws
10. Tax forms:
    a. Form SS-4 and Employer Identification Number
    b. Form 1023 or 1024
    c. Any State forms

Bank Account

A corporation will need a bank account. Checks payable to a corporation cannot be cashed by an individual; they must be deposited into a corporate account.

Fortunately, some banks have special rates for nonprofit organizations which are very reasonable.

All you should need to open a corporate bank account is a copy of your articles of incorporation and your federal tax identification number and perhaps a business license. Some banks, however, want more and they sometimes don't even know what they want. After opening numerous corporate accounts with only those items, one individual recently encountered a bank employee who wanted "something certified so we know who your officers are. Your attorney will know what to draw up." He explained that he was an attorney and was the president, secretary, and treasurer of the corporation and would write out and sign and seal whatever they wanted. The bank employee insisted that it had to be a nice certificate signed by the secretary of the corporation and sealed. So a statement was typed out in legalese, a gold foil seal was put on it, and the bank opened the account. If you have trouble opening the account you can use the "Banking Resolution" included with this book (appendix C), or you can make up a similar form.

LICENSES

In some states, counties and municipalities are authorized to levy a license fee or tax on the "privilege" of doing business. Nonprofit corporations do not always come under these laws, but some areas have registration provisions to keep track of nonprofits. Check with your town, city, or county clerk to see if registration is required.

As explained in chapter 6, if you will be doing charitable solicitations, many states will require you to register.

APPLYING FOR TAX EXEMPT STATUS 4

Although it is commonly thought that the Internal Revenue Service grants exemptions to nonprofit organizations, technically, the IRS merely checks to see whether an organization is exempt. The exemption has already been granted by Congress and the Service's only role is to recognize it.

Having your exemption recognized is an important and somewhat complicated process. You will need to read and understand the tax laws and correctly spell out a purpose for your organization which complies with the law.

If you know of any attorneys or accountants who offer low cost or free services to nonprofit organizations, you should consider using their services. They can save you a lot of time and frustration.

CHARITABLE ORGANIZATIONS

As explained earlier, under the tax law, the word charitable does not only mean charities which help the poor, it means any organizations which qualify to receive tax deductible donations. If at all possible, you should structure your organization as a charitable organization under IRS Code section 501(c)(3).

If you cannot, for example, if you plan to do substantial lobbying or to participate in political campaigns, you will need to form a noncharitable organization under another section of the IRC as explained in the next section.

FORMS

If you sent for the materials mentioned in chapter 3, you should have the forms and publications you will need which are:

☛ Package 1023 Application for Recognition of Exemption

☛ Form 8718 User Fee for Exempt Organization Determination Letter Request

☛ Publication 557

☛ Publication 578

Churches do not need to file the form. Organizations which receive less than $5,000 per year are not required to file, but they should file anyway for the following benefits:

☛ assures donors of deductibility of donations;

☛ allows exemption from state taxes;

☛ allows nonprofit postal rates; and

☛ the information from the form can be used later in other filings such as state exemption applications, grant applications, and the like.

Considering the complexity of the law, the instructions and publication are fairly well written. They guide you through the form, line-by-line, and refer to other sections of the IRC when necessary. If you are preparing your own application, be sure to read both the instructions and Publication 557 thoroughly before beginning. The following are important issues to consider on the more difficult questions on Form 1023.

Part I. This part is fairly straightforward. For line 2, if you do not yet have your EIN you can include form SS-4 with this application. For line 10, you do not need to send a certified or file-stamped copy, but if you do not, you need to attach a written declaration to the copies you send stating that they are "true and correct copies of the originals which are on file with the secretary of state."

Part II. This is the most important part and question 1 is the most important question. You should read IRS publication 557 and chapter 5 of this book before attempting this. If after reading these, you feel that your answer may be questionable, you should check with an attorney or research some of the additional references in appendix A of this book.

Line 2 is concerned with whether your organization is a public charity or private foundation. As explained in chapter 2, it is important to be a public charity so you must endeavor to pass either the public support or the facts and circumstances test.

On line 4c it looks better if an organization has a public official on its board but not necessary.

Line 4d is about *disqualified persons*. These are the people who started, control, or are major contributors to the organization and their family members. It is not a problem if these people are on the board or have relationships, but there will be a stricter scrutiny of the transactions to be sure there is not any excess benefit.

If you check yes to any question on lines 5, 6, or 7, you should consult with an attorney to be sure the arrangement is allowable.

For line 12a, it is okay if there are charges for the services (such as for museum entrance, copies of publications, etc.), but the basis of the fee should be to recover costs, not to make a profit. For line 12, it is better if the organization's benefits are available to the general public. If the benefits are limited to a certain group, that group must be a natural, reasonable limitation (such as limiting an animal shelter to one county, where there are existing groups operating in surrounding counties).

You can admit to "insubstantial" lobbying on line 13 (as explained in chapter 5); however, this just opens up a can of worms and as a new organization, you should stay away from lobbying until you have a clear budget and can pass the tests.

If you answer yes on line 14, your exemption will be denied.

Part III. This section answers technical requirements as to the effective date and whether the organization is a private foundation. Read Publication 557 and chapter 2 again before answering these questions.

Part IV. Unless you are incorporating an existing association, you will need to prepare proposed budgets rather than financial statements. You may wonder how you can possibly know where your money will come from if you have just started, but you can at least make preliminary plans based upon whether you will apply for grants or operate fundraising drives. It doesn't matter if your actual funding comes in different from your plan as long as you are still able to pass the tests avoiding private foundation status.

While filling out the forms, keep in mind that, under the law, they will be public record and anyone can get a copy of them from the IRS or from you. (There is a penalty if you do not provide copies to those who request them.) Therefore, if there is any information which you need to include on the form but wish to keep private (such as donor lists, trade secrets), you can put "See Attachment" in the space for the information on the form and then write on the attachment "NOT SUBJECT TO PUBLIC INSPECTION" and include the necessary information to be concealed, such as the trade secret. Then you should attach a statement of why the information would be withheld from the public.

NONCHARITABLE ORGANIZATIONS

If your organization cannot qualify as a charitable organization under section 501(c)(3), it will need to apply under a different section of the code and use a different packet of IRS forms.

Some of the other types on nonprofit organizations which can apply for tax exemption and the code sections which they must qualify under are:

Business leagues	§ 501(c)(6)
Chambers of commerce	§ 501(c)(6)

Civic leagues	§ 501(c)(4)
Employee associations	§ 501(c)(4), (9), or (17)
Labor organizations	§ 501(c)(5)
Lodges	§ 501(c)(10)
Recreational clubs	§ 501(c)(7)
Social clubs	§ 501(c)(7)
Social welfare organizations	§ 501(c)(4)
Veterans organizations	§ 501(c)(19)

All of these organizations would use Package 1024 (rather than 1023) to apply for recognition of their tax exemption. The questions are similar to those discussed above for charitable organizations, but the rules are not as strict. The main concern is that none of the directors or members receive any financial benefits from the organization. If some of them receive salaries or rents from the organization, the rates must be reasonable and no higher than would be paid to a third party.

SUBMITTING YOUR APPLICATION

The forms should be filed within fifteen months after incorporation in order to have the tax exempt status apply from your corporation's beginning. If the forms are late, they only apply from the date of filing. However, you can get an extension if you ask before the the end of the fifteen months.

Along with your application, you will need to include form 8718 (User Fee for Exempt Organization Determination Letter), financial statements for the previous three years (or proposed budgets for the next two), and copies of the corporation's articles of organization and bylaws. The copy of the articles must be conformed, meaning an exact copy. It is best to send a photocopy of a copy which has been date-stamped or certified by the Secretary of State. Otherwise, you may need to include a written declaration certifying its authenticity as explained in the instructions. The copy of the bylaws need not be signed if they are submitted as an attachment to the form 1023.

RESPONSE TO YOUR APPLICATION

The response by the IRS to your application can be a yes, no, or maybe. If you have successfully completed the form to the satisfaction of the IRS, your exemption will be granted. If they are not sure your organization qualifies, they may ask for clarifications or more information. If it appears from your application that your group does not qualify, they will issue a "proposed adverse determination." You have thirty days to appeal this ruling before it becomes final. For information of how to appeal, you should get IRS Publication 892, *Exempt Organization Appeal Procedures for Unagreed Issues.*

STATE TAX EXEMPTIONS

Most states also exempt many types of nonprofit organizations from income, property, sales, and other types of taxes. In most states, the exemption is automatic either because the organization is formed as a nonprofit or the organization's exemption is recognized by the IRS.

On the state pages in appendix B are the addresses of the state departments of revenue and whether the exemption is automatic or not. You should write to the department and ask for the forms necessary for the state exemptions.

PROTECTING YOUR NONPROFIT STATUS

5

The rules are strict for nonprofit corporations and if they are broken, tax exempt status can be lost and additional taxes and penalties can be owed. This chapter explains the most important rules and how to avoid breaking them.

PRIVATE INUREMENT

The *private inurement doctrine* is one of the most important concepts of nonprofit law. It is the rule that the funds and benefits of a nonprofit organization cannot go to any particular persons but must be used for the approved purpose of the organization. The rule was meant to keep people from using the form of a nonprofit organization to avoid taxes for private transactions such as when a wealthy individual started a foundation to hire his relatives instead of give them taxable gifts or inheritances.

The rule doesn't seem to make sense for organizations such as social clubs or a trade associations whose whole purpose in being is to give benefits to their members rather than society. For these organizations, the law contorts itself to say that, the members can benefit from the organization, but only if all the members benefit, not just some of them. Also, these groups are limited in how much of their funds can come from outside the group. Dues and contributions from members are not taxable, but if they raise too much money from outsiders, that income may be taxable.

To help you understand what the private inurement requires, here are some examples:

- ☞ A trade association can be formed by apple growers to promote the eating of apples, but it cannot only work to sell its members apples. It must promote the eating of apples in general.

- ☞ A social club can be set up for the benefit of an ethnic group, such as an Italian-Americans club. But it cannot give special benefits to some members such as reduced dues which are subsidized by other members.

- ☞ A scientific organization can be formed to test electrical products for safety, but it cannot work for the interests of just a few manufacturers.

- ☞ A museum can be set up to display and sell works of art, but not if its purpose is selling it's members' works for their financial gain.

EXCESS BENEFITS TRANSACTIONS

Besides not having the purpose of the organization to benefit private parties, the actual operations of the group must not give excess profits to private individuals.

Nonprofit organizations are allowed to hire employees, rent property, and pay for services, and in most cases, there is not a prohibition against hiring, renting from, or buying from their own directors or officers—as long as it is a fair transaction. But the salary must not exceed what is fair in the community, the rent must be fair market rent, and the services must not be overpriced compared to other providers of the same services.

Transactions between nonprofits and their directors, officers, and members will be looked at carefully by the IRS, so you should keep careful records and be able to back up all transactions. For example, if a director rents office space to an organization, you should have evidence of what rents are charged to others and what other rentals are available to the organization. If the organization pays salaries to employees and officers, you should document what those people have earned elsewhere and what similar organizations are paying similar employees.

LOBBYING

PUBLIC
CHARITIES

The basic rule for charitable nonprofit corporations is that if a *substantial part* of the activities consist of *propaganda* or *attempting to influence legislation*, then the tax exemption will be denied or revoked.

One might think that it would be natural for a nonprofit organization to support laws which aid its mission and in fact for a long time this was allowed, until one group upset some U.S. Senators and without any hearings, they got a law passed which forbids substantial lobbying.

Lobbying is generally considered to be either directly contacting legislators to influence legislation or attempting to influence public opinion on an issue of legislation. It is not considered lobbying merely to do a nonpartisan study or analysis or to respond to legislative requests for information.

What exactly constitutes *substantial* in the case of lobbying has been a contentious issue for a long time. After years of fighting between Congress, the IRS, and nonprofits, there are presently two tests which can be used by a nonprofit to be sure it is not violating the limit, the *substantial part test* and the *expenditures test*. All charities must pass the substantial part test unless they elect to use the expenditures test. Churches and their related organizations are not allowed to elect the expenditures test.

The expenditures test was devised because the substantial part test was so difficult to understand and there were no strict standards to guide the IRS agents. The basic rule of the substantial part test is that no more than fifteen percent of the organization's expenditures can be for lobbying. However, the fact that it is hard to put a dollar value on many actions of an organization makes it easy for an organization to err. For example, how much money was expended if a group puts one paragraph in their newsletter promoting a legislative issue? Would you include a percentage of the printing, postage, and addressing, as well as the office rent and utilities?

Although the expenditures test was meant to give organizations some certainty, few have used it because the IRS rules require much greater record keeping. The basic rule is that an organization is allowed to spend twenty percent of its first $500,000 on exempt purpose expenditures, fifteen percent of the next $500,000, ten percent of the next $1,000,000 and five percent of the rest. However, no group can spend more than $1,000,000 on lobbying. To make the election, the organization files IRS Form 5768 and must use Part VI-A of Schedule A, Form 990, to figure the limits.

PRIVATE FOUNDATIONS

Private foundations under § 501(c)(3) are not permitted to do any lobbying at all.

OTHER NONPROFITS

Nonprofit organizations which are exempt under provisions other than § 501(c)(3), such as social welfare organizations and trade associations, are not limited in the lobbying they can do. Thus, many charitable nonprofit organizations set up noncharitable nonprofit organizations to handle the lobbying in which they are interested.

PENALTY

The penalty for violation of these rules can be a tax on the amounts expended or complete loss of tax exempt status.

FURTHER INFORMATION

The Nonprofit Lobbying Guide is an excellent book which explains in detail the legislative process and how a nonprofit organization can lobby successfully and legally. It is available for $16 from Independent Sector (1-888-860-8118) or in PDF format at no charge at:

http://indepsec.org/media/Nonprofit_LobbyingGuide_Release.html

POLITICAL CAMPAIGNING

Political campaigning is even more strictly controlled for nonprofits. Political campaigning is considered the support of particular candidates for office, (as opposed to lobbying which is support of legislation). The general rule is that charitable organizations may not do any political campaigning and noncharitable nonprofits can only do limited campaigning, but special organizations known as political action committees (PACs) can be set up to solely do political campaigning. Like the restriction on lobbying, this rule came about because one U.S. Senator was upset that a charitable organization was campaigning against him.

Like the rules against lobbying, these allow an organization to do non-partisan voter information campaigns. For example, a group could send out pamphlets listing how legislators voted on particular issues, such as gun control and abortion, without being considered supporting any particular candidates. However, the pamphlets are supposed to be written in a nonpartisan manner without indicating approval or disapproval of either record.

OTHER NONPROFITS
Although the tax law does not impose an absolute ban on political campaigning by nonprofits which are not charitable, federal election laws severely limit what nonprofit corporations can do. This is the reason why most nonprofit corporations that wish to participate in campaigns set up PACs for the purpose of poltical campaigning.

PENALTY
The penalty for violation of these rules can be a tax on the amounts expended or complete loss of tax exempt status.

CONFLICTS OF INTEREST AND SELF-DEALING

It is not fatal for an organization to have dealings with its insiders (disqualified persons in IRS parlance), but it requires careful documentation and at times can look bad to outsiders. As discussed above, any transactions with insiders should be documented.

You should also keep in mind that conflicts of interest or *nepotism* in an organization can have a negative effect on members or contributors. If the person who starts an organization hires all of his family members and no one else to work for the organization, it may be seen as a conflict of interest to those who make grants or want to join. In some cases, where the organization is doing a clear good, the salaries are below normal, and few other people are willing to get involved, this may not be a problem. But in a large organization where many people want to be involved, it may cause political problems resulting in a loss of support and even the formation of splinter groups.

One thing you must avoid is keeping any conflicts in secret. If the organization is dealing with an insider or an insider's family member, don't try to hide it. Explain the relationship and put it in the records.

SOURCES OF INCOME

There are two main concerns of nonprofit organizations when it comes to the sources if income. The first is that new funds coming in do not cause it to lose its public charity status, and the second is that not too much of the money is from sources unrelated to its exempt function.

DONATIONS
As explained in chapter 2 a charitable nonprofit organization does not want to be a private foundation. The only way it can do this is to pass one of the tests based on the source of its income. It must be sure that its income comes from "public" sources rather than one or two rich donors. Keep these tests in mind when raising money. This may mean declining certain donations if they would threaten your status.

FUNDRAISING ACTIVITIES
Both charitable and noncharitable organizations must be careful about how they earn money. If too much comes from improper sources, they may be required to pay tax penalties or completely lose their tax

exemption. For charitable organizations, the basic rule is that the money making activities must be related to the exempt function of the organization. For noncharitable organizations, only a limited amount may be raised from nonmembers. More information on raising money is contained in the next chapter.

CHECKLIST FOR AVOIDING PROBLEMS

- Dealings with insiders

    ☐ Be sure the amount is reasonable

    ☐ Keep detailed documentation

    ☐ Be open/ No hidden deals

- Lobbying

    ☐ Charitable organizations: only insubstantial

    ☐ Set up a separate organization if necessary

    ☐ Noncharitable organizations: okay but not deductible

- Political campaigning

    ☐ No political campaigning

    ☐ Only nonpartisan voter education

    ☐ Set up a PAC for campaigning.

- Sources of income

    ☐ Watch public support limits

    ☐ Limit unrelated income

    ☐ Pay taxes on unrelated income

Raising Money in a Nonprofit Corporation 6

A nonprofit organization cannot operate like a profit making business. It is limited to the types of profit-making operations it may run. But it has other possibilities for making money which are not open to profit making companies.

Applying for Grants

One of the main benefits of a nonprofit corporation is that it can qualify for grants from both private foundations and government agencies. There are thousands of grants available through various programs, some of which have no one claiming them. If you do your homework you may be able to qualify for the fund you need to run your programs.

Getting a grant is not always easy, however. If you do not answer the questions correctly or provide the required documentation you will not get the grants. Writing grant applications has become a profession in itself and there are those who do nothing but compile the right information needed for organizations to qualify for grants.

As a new organization you will probably not want to start using expensive grant-writing services just yet. It will be a good educational experience for you to make some grant applications to learn the process. Grant applications are like tax returns in that you can better use the services of a professional if you have done it once yourself and know what kind of information will be needed.

Fortunately there are many organizations whose purpose it is to help individuals and organizations learn how to apply for grants. One of the best is The Foundation Center. This organization compiles information about all of the foundations which make grants and makes it available in books, libraries and their web site. They have five centers, in Atlanta, Cleveland, New York, San Francisco and Washington, and sponsor collections of foundation materials in two hundred libraries around the country. To locate their publications check their website, http://www.fdncenter.org/, or the largest library near you. Some of their publications include:

The Foundation Directory
Guide to U.S. Foundations, Their Trustees, Officers, and Donors
National Directory of Corporate Giving
Corporate Foundation Profiles
National Guide to Funding in Arts and Culture
National Guide to Funding for Community Development
National Guide to Funding for the Environment and Animal Welfare
National Guide to Funding in Health
AIDS Fundraising
National Guide to Funding for Information Technology
National Guide to Funding for Women and Girls

For beginners they have a grant tutorial which explains how to research and apply for grants. It can be found at: http://fdncenter.org/onlib/orient/intro1.html.

SOLICITING DONATIONS

For nonprofit organizations which cannot get grants, or are intimidated with the application process, the primary source of funding is solicitation of donations from the public.

For organizations which qualify under IRC § 501(c)(3) as charitable, the donation is tax deductible to the giver. However, if a donor receives something for his or her donation, then only the amount in excess of the value of the item is deductible. For example, if an organization holds a fundraising dinner at $100 a plate, and the value of the dinner is $25, then only $75 of the payment is tax deductible. Because of abuses in this area, the IRS has begun requiring nonprofits to tell donors what portion of their payment is deductible.

Donations to other nonprofit organizations (social welfare, business leagues, etc.) are not deductible unless they are legitimate business expenses. Donations made to an organization (such as a trade association) which are normally deductible as business expenses are limited if the organization engages in lobbying. An organization which engages in lobbying must keep a record of what portion of its budget is used for lobbying and let members know that this portion is not tax deductible.

Organizations should keep in mind that besides soliciting immediate gifts from the public, they should also look for bequests in peoples' wills. People who might only make small donations during their lifetime might be willing to make much greater contributions to causes they believe in once they no longer have a need for the money. This is especially true of those with large estates and few or no children.

There are additional tax benefits for bequests to charity and complicated schemes to allow the givers to enjoy the income from their gift during their life while allowing the remainder to go to charity.

CHARITABLE SOLICITATION LAWS

Because of abuses and outright fraud by some nonprofits in the past, there are now numerous laws regulating the solicitation of money for charitable purposes. The federal, state, and many local governments have gotten into the act to protect the public from abuses.

If you will be asking for donations from the public, you will need to comply with these laws or face civil or even criminal penalties. In many states, your organization must register before it can begin solicitations. If you plan a national solicitation campaign, you will need to learn the laws of all fifty states.

Fortunately, there is a movement to simplify the process. A uniform registration form has been proposed and accepted by many states. Also, there is a lot of guidance available to nonprofits, much of it free.

Because of our constitutional guarantee of free speech, the regulation of fundraising by nonprofit organizations must be very narrowly drawn. Nonprofits are not considered commercial enterprises, so the regulation of them cannot be so broad. But the regulation that has been allowed is still a substantial burden and requires strict compliance.

FEDERAL LAWS   Federal laws concerned with charitable solicitations mostly cover the tax aspects. The biggest abuse in this area is when donors are lead to believe that their payments to organizations are deductible when they are not.

One requirement is that groups to which donations are not deductible must state in their solicitation that payments are not deductible as charitable contributions for federal income tax purposes. This rule does not apply to groups whose gross receipts are less than $100,000 a year or if the solicitation goes to less than ten people or only by face-to-face solicitations. The penalty can be up to $10,000 if the violation was unintentional or fifty percent of the money collected if intentional.

Although donations to nonqualified groups are not deductible as charitable contributions, in some cases, they may be deducted as business expenses. For example, a real estate agent may deduct dues to a real estate board. However, any part of the dues which are used to lobby the government are not deductible and organizations which are exempt under sections 501(c)(4), (5) and (6) must make their members aware of what amount is not deductible.

For groups to which donations are deductible, the three main rules are that when a donee gets something in exchange for their gift, only an amount in excess of the fair value of the premium is deductible; when the amount is over $75, the donee must be given a written statement indicating what amount is deductible; and when a donation is over $250, a written receipt must be given to the donor. See IRS publications 526 and 557.

STATE LAWS
The biggest burden on fundraising by nonprofits is that most states require registration and disclosure and some require filing fees or bonds which cost hundreds of dollars. For national organizations, it is a considerable burden to keep track of the laws in all fifty states, send for the filing forms, keep track of all the different deadlines, and compile all the required information. For small nonprofits just starting out, it is practically impossible.

What to do if you are a new organization which needs to raise funds? First, you could see if you are exempt. Each state has different categories of groups that are exempt. Exempt groups typically include religious organizations, schools, hospitals, and some clubs. Also, most states have a dollar limit such as $10,000 or $25,000. You are exempt until your donations reach that level. The dollar limits that are exempt for each state are included in appendix B. However, since the laws often change, you should check to be sure the figures are current. One good place to find information on state requirements is the following website: http://www.raffa.com.

If you do not come under any of these exemptions, you will need to consider registration. If you will be doing most of your fundraising in your own state, you should start by getting that registration information (if registration is required in your state) and learn the system by complying with those regulations. Next, you could expand your fundraising into the states which do not have registration requirements. These are:

Delaware	Nebraska
Hawaii	Nevada
Idaho	South Dakota (telephone sol. must reg.)
Indiana	Texas
Iowa	Vermont
Montana	Wyoming

Your next step could be to start registering on a state-by-state basis. If your potential donors are concentrated in a few states, then, of course, those would be the best ones with which to start. If not, you could start with the states with the simplest or cheapest registration or the states with the highest population.

Just as there is a big difference in what each state requires, there is also a difference on how seriously a state keeps track of its registrations. Some states demand strict compliance and have teams of attorneys investigating nonprofit compliance, others just pile the registration forms in a warehouse. If you find that strict compliance is not possible because of your group's limited resources, here are some things to consider.

The United States Supreme Court has ruled that states do not have the right to require companies to collect sales taxes if they do not do business in that state. Mailing catalogs to and placing advertisements in a state is not considered enough to be doing business. Some have argued that merely mailing charitable solicitations to people in a state is not enough to allow the state to require registration and a court case is being considered.

Your group could take the position that sending a few solicitations by mail to a state is not enough to require your registration. Most likely, your letters would not be brought to the attention of the regulators any-way. However, if they do find out about you and do decide that you should have registered, you may end up paying legal fees to resolve the matter. If your promotional materials are honest and you use the funds legitimately, you will be in much better position than if your materials are misleading and your promotion is a scam!

The Internet has added new legal issues to the matter of charitable solicitations. A few misguided courts have ruled that anyone who has a website is legally "doing business" in any place which can view the site. This has lead to some ridiculous conclusions such as a New York web-site owner can be guilty of the crime of violating German obscenity law.

If this rationale is accepted, the strictest law of any town on the planet would control every site on the Internet—clearly, an unworkable sys-tem. Therefore, states that insist that anyone with a website comes under their jurisdiction are most likely wrong, and soliciting funds on your website should not bring you under the jurisdiction of all fifty states. However, keep in mind that the law is not yet clear on this point and some states insist that it does.

If you are registered in some states and not others, you could put a disclaimer on your website that it is only intended for residents of those states. This should protect you, but as the law is so new and still in flux you can't yet be sure in every case.

UNIFORM REGISTRATION STATEMENT

Because the different registration requirements of the different states create such a burden on interstate nonprofit organizations, there has been an effort by many of them to standardize the process. Instead of a different form with different requirements for each state, they have pro-posed a Uniform Registration Statement which could be used for all states.

Not all states have agreed to this since it has to go through hearings in each state legislature. But many states have, and, in time, there may be just one form for all states.

At this point the following states have agreed to accept the URS.

Alabama	Maryland	New Jersey
Arkansas	Massachusetts	New Mexico
California	Michigan	New York
Connecticut	Minnesota	North Dakota
D.C.	Mississippi	Pennsylvania
Georgia	Missouri	Rhode Island
Illinois	Ohio	South Carolina
Kansas	Oklahoma	Tennessee
Kentucky	Oregon	Virginia
Louisiana	Nebraska	Washington
Maine	New Hampshire	

LOCAL LAWS

Besides the state laws, numerous cities and towns have their own charitable solicitation laws. While many of these only apply to in-person, door-to-door, or telephone solicitors, some expect every group conducting a national campaign to register.

If you are conducting a local fundraising campaign, you should check with the clerk of any city or town in which you'll be operating. Checking with every town in the nation is clearly beyond the ability of most new groups. When you grow, you may need to hire a professional fundraiser who can keep track of such compliance.

CONSTITUTIONAL ISSUES

The area of regulation of charitable solicitations raises some serious constitutional issues, most importantly, free speech. While states have argued that soliciting money is a commercial activity which is subject to regulation, the United States Supreme Court has held that asking for money for charitable causes is *not* commercial speech but is a highly protected form of free speech.

Whereas most laws only need to be reasonable to be valid, any laws which regulate charitable fundraising must be as limited as possible to achieve only a legitimate and narrow governmental interest. They cannot use broad formulas, such as percentages of net proceeds that go to charity, to limit solicitations and they cannot require lengthy disclosures to be made during verbal solicitations.

Unfortunately, state legislatures, up in arms about some recent abuse, often ignore their citizens' federal constitutional rights. Many laws have been passed in this area which were not legal, and the only way to avoid the penalties was to go to court. And many of the laws on the books today would not be upheld if taken to court.

If you, in good faith, feel that a regulation violates your constitutional rights, you can ignore it. However, keep in mind that if someone complains, and if you are investigated and charged with violation of the law, you will need to take the time and money to defend yourself or face the penalties.

Three areas which states have ben able to regulate are when there is trespassing, gambling, fraud and disclosure. Laws on these subjects which affect charitable solicitors will usually be upheld if they are reasonable.

Unrelated Business Income

To keep nonprofit organizations from competing unfairly with profit-making businesses, there are strict limits on how much unrelated income such groups can have. Violation of the limits can result in tax penalties or loss of tax-exempt status. In all cases, unrelated business income is taxed and a separate tax form must be filed for the taxable income.

There are some exemptions and safe harbors for nonprofits, which allow income to be raised without penalty. The rule is that an organization cannot regularly operate an unrelated trade or business. Both of these requirements offer a safe harbor. If an organization operates a business only sporadically, such as an annual fund drive, the income is exempt. If the business is related to its exempt function, such as a cafeteria in a hospital or a bookstore in a school, that is exempt.

EXEMPT
ACTIVITIES

Besides the exemptions explained above for related and sporadic income sources, there are some exempt types of income which nonprofit organizations can earn without penalty. These include:

☞ Activities carried on primarily for the benefit of the members, employees, patients, students or officers of the organization.

☞ Activities done by volunteers, such as a car wash, carnival, or Christmas tree sale.

☞ Renting out the organization's list of donors.

☞ Selling items donated to the organization such as a bake sale, book sale, or thrift shop.

☞ Low cost items given for donations, such as address labels, Christmas seals, or greeting cards.

☞ Trade shows about the organization's exempt function.

☞ Interest, dividends, royalties.

☞ Rents.

☞ Profits on sale of property owned by the organization.

ASSOCIATE
MEMBERS

In recent years, the IRS has cracked down on organizations which have different classes of members. Typically, a tax exempt group will have regular members and associate members which do not usually partici-pate in the group in the same as regular members but get many of the same benefits. The current position of the IRS is that if the rights and participation between different classes of members are too different, then the associates' member dues are unrelated business taxable income. For guidance, see IRS Rev. Proc. 95-21.

AFFINITY
PROGRAMS

A relatively recent way for nonprofits to earn extra income is to endorse certain products, such as car rental companies or long distance carriers, to their members and get a percentage of the income generated. Some groups sponsor their own credit cards with the symbols of their organization appearing on the card.

Such arrangements can either be unrelated business taxable income or exempt royalty income, depending on how the deal is structured. If it is a passive arrangement where the group merely receives a royalty for use of its logo, the income is passive and nontaxable. If the members of the group must materially participate, such as in promoting the products, the income is then taxable. For guidance, see. IRS Rev. Rul. 81-178, 1981-2 C.B. 135.

CORPORATE SPONSORSHIP

Income received from corporations in sponsorship of events run by nonprofit corporations may or may not be taxable depending on whether the corporate sponsor is *promoted* or merely identified at the event. Displaying a brand, logo, or name of a sponsor; listing products or services; or giving addresses or phone numbers is allowable as mere identification. But promoting products, giving prices or discounts, or suggesting people buy the products is considered promotions and any money received for them is taxable. For guidance, see IRS Prop. Reg. 1.513-4.

RUNNING A NONPROFIT CORPORATION 7

DAY TO DAY ACTIVITIES

On a day-to-day basis, there are not many differences between running a nonprofit corporation and any other type of business or corporation. The most important things to remember are the prohibitions explained in chapter 5. Make sure that everyone in the organization is aware of these, so that there are no slip-ups.

The prohibition on mixing personal and business matters in a for-profit corporation is even stronger for a nonprofit. Don't write corporation checks for your personal expenses, even if you pay them back quickly. Don't do favors for relatives with corporation assets. Treat the corporation as something you are responsible for taking care of for someone else.

Another important thing to remember is to always refer to the corporation as a corporation. *Always* use the complete corporate name including designations such as "Inc." or "Assn." *Always* sign corporate documents with your corporate title. If you don't, you may lose your protection from liability. There have been many cases where people forgot to put the word "president" after their name when entering into contracts for the corporation. As a result, they were determined to be personally liable for performance of the contract.

As explained in chapter 3, you should obtain a copy of your state's non-profit corporation laws and become familiar with them. Some states have specific requirements which must be complied with and you will be expected to know what is required of your organization

CORPORATE RECORDS

The laws on what types of records must be kept are slightly different in each state. You should review your state statute and make a list of what records are required and keep them all together with the list. The following are some typical rules.

ARTICLES AND
BYLAWS

Copies of the articles of organization, bylaws, and any revisions thereto must be kept on hand by the corporation

MINUTES

A corporation must keep minutes of the proceedings of its board of directors, members (if any), and any committees. The minutes should be in writing. Some states allow minutes to be kept in forms other than writing provided they can be converted into written form within a reasonable time. This would mean that they could be kept in a computer or possibly on a videotape. However, it is always best to keep a duplicate copy or at least one written copy. Accidents can easily erase magnetic media. Blank forms which can be used for regular minutes are included in appendix C of this book.

FINANCES

A nonprofit corporation must keep accurate financial records, especially if it is engaged in charitable solicitations. These records usually include records of all receipts and disbursements as well as tax returns and any other financial reports which are filed.

MEMBERS

If the corporation has members, it must usually keep accurate records of the names and addresses of the members. Some states require them to be in alphabetical order.

MEETINGS

The corporation must hold an annual meeting of the board of directors. If there are formal members, there must be a meeting of them as well. Usually, the members elect directors and the directors elect officers. Minutes of these meetings must be kept with the corporate records. Forms for the minutes of the annual meetings are included with this book. You can use them as master copies to photocopy each year. All that needs to be changed is the date, unless you actually change officers or directors or need to take some other corporate action.

ANNUAL REPORTS

CORPORATE

Most states require that every corporation must file an annual report. Some states want them only every two years. Fortunately, this is a simple, often one-page, form which is sent to the corporation by the Secretary of State and may merely need to be signed and dated. It contains such information as the federal tax identification number, officers' and directors' names and addresses, the registered agent's name and the address of the registered office. It must be signed and returned with the required fee by the date specified. If it is not, the corporation is dissolved after notice is given.

CHARITABLE SOLICITATION

Most states that require registration for charitable solicitation also require annual reports and some require detailed financial reports. The state pages in appendix B tell whether an annual report is required and provide the address to which you can write for more information.

TAX RETURNS

FEDERAL
Annual returns. Most nonprofit corporations are required to file a form 990 tax return each year. If the income is below $100,000 and assets below $250,000, then form 990EZ can be filed. If the income is less than $25,000 or the corporation is a church, school, or related organization, it may be exempt from filing. Check the instructions for the latest Form 990 to see if you qualify as exempt.

If your organization is a private foundation or has unrelated business income, you may need to file form 990-PF or 990-T. If a charitable organization makes a political contribution of over $100, it must file Form 1120-POL. Check the instructions for these forms or Publication 598 if these may apply to you.

Interim reports. In some cases, nonprofit corporations must file interim tax returns. If a charitable nonprofit organization receives a donation of certain types of property and sells or disposes of it within two years, the organization must file form 8282 with the IRS and give a copy to the donor. Also form 8300 must be filed if more than $10,000 in cash is received.

All organizations which have employees must make regular deposits of taxes withheld (quarterly or more often depending on the amount), and form 941 must be filed quarterly reporting these deposits.

STATE
Some states require annual filings by nonprofits, some waive them once they are exempt and others just want copies of the federal return. The addresses and phone numbers of the state revenue offices are listed in the state pages of appendix B.

EMPLOYMENT REQUIREMENTS

If you will be paying wages to anyone, even just yourself, you will need to comply with all of the employer reporting and withholding laws of both your state and the federal government. Explaining every requirement is beyond the scope of this book, but the following is a summary of most of the requirements.

New hire reporting. To improve the enforcement of child support payments, all employers must report the hiring of each new employee to an agency in the state.

Employment eligibility. To combat the hiring of illegal immigrants, employers must complete the Department of Justice form I-9 for each employee.

Federal tax withholding. Social security and income taxes must be withheld from employees' wages and deposited to an authorized bank quarterly, monthly, or more often depending on the amount. The initial step is to obtain a form W-4 from each employee upon hiring. (This same form can also be used to fulfill the new hire reporting law discussed previously.)

State withholding. In states that have income taxes, there is usually a withholding and reporting requirement similar to the federal one.

Local withholding. In cities that have income taxes, there is usually a withholding and reporting requirement similar to the federal one.

Unemployment compensation. There are taxes on employee wages (which employers must pay) which must be paid to the state and federal governments regularly. Also, employers are required to submit reports both quarterly and annually.

Workers' compensation. Depending on the number of employees and the type of work, the state may require that workers' compensation insurance be obtained by the employer.

TRAINING

There are many training programs and manuals available to nonprofit organizations and if you, your board of directors, and officers are new to the world of nonprofits, you should consider them. Many of the resources in the next chapter sponsor programs, publish manuals, and have educational websites. Because the rules for nonprofits are different than from for-profit businesses, you should encourage everyone in your group to learn as much as possible. If many of them aren't able to go, you can go yourself and then hold training sessions for them.

APPENDIX A
RESOURCES FOR
NONPROFIT ORGANIZATIONS

This appendix includes organizations, websites and books which offer useful information to nonprofit organizations.

Organizations

Alliance of Nonprofit Mailers
1211 Connecticut Ave NW #620
Washington, DC 20036-2701
202-462-5132
www.nonprofitmailers.org

The Aspen Institute
1333 New Hampshire Ave., NW #1070
Washington, DC 20036
202-736-5838

Accounting Aid Society
One Kennedy Square
719 Griswold, #2026
Detroit, MI 48226
313-961-1840

The Foundation Center
79 Fifth Avenue
Nw York, NY 10003
800-424-9836
www.fdncenter.org

National Center for Nonprofit Boards
2000 L Street, NW #510
Washington, DC 20036
800-883-6262

National Council of Nonprofit Assns.
1900 L Street, NW
Washington, DC 20036
202-467-6262

Websites

Grant Writers Assistant
  http://fallingrock.com/GWA/LINKS/HOTLINKS

University of Wisconsin - Madison Resources for starting a nonprofit
  http://w.library.wisc.edu/libraries/Memorial/grants/npweb.htm

Council on Foundations
  http://www.cof.org

Thompson & Thompson, P.C. Nonprofit Tax issues
  http://www.taxexemptlaw.com/

Internal Revenue Service
  http://www.irs.ustreas.gov/prod/bus_info/eo/

The Nonprofit Resource Center
  http://www.not-for-profit.or

Internet Nonprofit Center
  http://www.nonprofits.org

Nonprofit Development Center
  http://www.npdc.org

Center for Excellence in Nonprofits
  http://www.cen.org

Books

The following books provide detailed information on all aspects of nonprofit organization law. If you have a specific question, you may find the answer in these. However, some of them cost over a hundred dollars, so you might want to review them at a law library if you are new and on a limited budget.

Nonprofit Law Dictionary, Hopkins, Bruce R., Wiley, John, & Sons, Inc.

Parliamentary Law and Practice for Nonprofit Organizations, Oleck, Howard L. & Green, Cami, ALI-ABA, 1994

The Legal Answer Book for Nonprofit Organizations, Hopkins, Bruce R., Wiley, John, & Sons, Inc., 1996

The Second Legal Answer Book for Nonprofit Organizations, Hopkins, Bruce R., Wiley, John, & Sons, Inc., 1999

Nonprofit Enterprises: Law and Taxation, Phelan, Marilyn E., Callaghan

Nonprofit Corporations, Organizations & Associations, Oleck, Howard L. and Stewart, Martha E., Prentice Hall

The following books are available from The Foundation Center:

America's Nonprofit Sector: A Primer

Best Practices of Effective Nonprofit Organizations

The Board Member's Book

The Handbook on Private Foundations

The Nonprofit Entrepreneur

Promoting Issues and Ideas

The 21st Century Nonprofit

Online Newsletters

Nonprofit Times
http://www.nptimes.org
Don Kramer's Nonprofit Issues
http://www.nonprofitissues.com

APPENDIX B
STATE-BY-STATE NONPROFIT
LAWS AND ADDRESSES

The following pages contain a listing of each state's non-profit corporation laws and fees. Because the laws are constantly being changed by state legislatures, you should call before filing your papers to confirm the fees and other requirements. The phone numbers are provided for each state.

In the continued growth of the world wide web, more and more state corporation divisions are making their fees and procedures available online. Some states have downloadable forms available and some even allow you to search their entire database from the comfort of your home or office.

The best websites at the time of publication of this book are included for each state. However, the sites change constantly so you may need to look a little deeper if your state's site has changed its address.

Acknowledgement

Special thanks must be given to Oliver Stutz, Jens Werner, and Karoline Fiedler, our legal interns, who worked long hours compiling the data in this appendix from the law libraries, the Internet, and letters to the various offices.

ALABAMA

INCORPORATION:

Secretary of State
Corporate Section
P.O. Box 5616
Montgomery, AL 36130-5616
Tel: 334-242-5324
Website:
www.sos.state.al.us/business/corporat.htm

What they supply:

State provides fill-in-the-blanks-Articles of Incorporation with instructions. You can download the form from the Internet (www.sos.state.al.us/download/business/). The Adobe® Acrobat Reader™ is required for a successful download.

What must be filed:

At first you have to secure a name reservation from the Secretary of State for the proposed corporate name. After successful reservation you have to file the Articles of Incorporation at the Judge of Probate office in the county where the corporation's registered office is located. Please enclose two copies of the articles and one copy of the name reservation.

Name requirements:

The corporate name shall not be the same, or deceptively similar, to the name of any other corporation existing in Alabama. The name may not contain a word or phrase which indicates that it is organized for a purpose other than contained in the Articles of Incorporation.

Directors requirements:

Your Corporation must be have at least three directors. You have to fix the number of directors by the bylaws. The directors may be divided in classes and the terms of the different classes need not to be uniform.

Articles requirements:

The minimum requirements are as follows:
- the name of the corporation
- the period of duration
- the purpose of the corporation

- any provisions for the regulation of the internal affairs (including final liquidation)
- local and mailing address
- number of the directors constituting the initial board of directors and names and addresses of the initial directors.
- name and address of each incorporator

Filing fees:

The Judge of Probate filing fee is $25 and the Secretary of State's fee is $20. Both fees are payable to the Judge of Probate.

Reports:

You have to file an annual report between January 1 and March 15.

Statute: Alabama Code 10-3A-1 to 225

TAXES:

Alabama Department of Revenue
Corporate Section
P.O. Box 327310
Montgomery, AL 36132-7310
Tel: 334-242-2000
Website: http://www.ador.state.al.us

Automatic Exemption: No

CHARITABLE SOLICITATION:

Attorney General
Consumer protection Division
11 S. Union Street
Montgomery, AL 36130
Tel: (334) 242-7334

Statute: Alabama Code 13A-9-70, et seq.

Exemption:

less than $25,000, provided that all fundraising functions are carried out by volunteers

Annual filing: Yes

Accept URS: Yes

ALASKA

INCORPORATION:

Dept. of Commerce and Economic Dev.
Attention: Corporation Section
P.O. Box 110807
Juneau, AK 99811-0807
Tel: 907-465-2521
Fax: 907-465-2549
Website: www.commerce.state.ak.us/

What they supply:

State provides fill-in-the-blanks Articles of Incorporation with instructions and information about nonprofit corporations.

What must be filed:

Print or type your documents in black ink and file two copies of the Articles of Incorporation. Make sure your documents bear the original signatures and are both notarized. Enclose the filing fee. One copy will be returned to you for your records.

Name Requirements:

The corporate name may not contain a word or phrase which indicates or implies that it is organized for a purpose other than one or more of the purposes contained in your Articles of Incorporation.

Directors Requirements:

Your nonprofit corporation must have at least three initial directors. The number of directors has to be fixed by the Bylaws later on but the initial board of directors shall be fixed by the Articles of Incorporation. The directors don't have to be residents of Alaska or members of the corporation, unless your Articles or Bylaws require so. The director's default term is one year.

Articles requirements:

You must state the names and addresses of your first board of directors in Article 6. In Alaska there must be at least three incorporators who must be natural persons at least 19 years old. Enter the names and (business) addresses of these incorporators in Article 7. Make sure that your Articles are notarized.

Filing fees:

$50, payable to the Alaska Department of Commerce and Economic Development.

Reports: You have to file an annual report by July 2.

Statute: Alaska Statutes, Section 10.06.208-210

TAXES:

Alaska Department of Revenue
P.O. Box SA
Juneau, AK 99811-0400
Tel: 907-465-2372
Fax: 907-465-2389
Website: http://www.revenue.state.ak.us/

Automatic Exemption: Yes

CHARITABLE SOLICITATION:

Department of Law
Fair Business Practices Section
1031 W. 4th Ave #200
Anchorage, AK 99501-1994
Tel.: 907-269-5100

Statute: Alaska Statutes, Title 45, Chapter 68

Exemption: First $5.000 or 10 or less donors

Annual filing: Yes

Accept URS: No

ARIZONA

INCORPORATION:

Arizona Corporation Commission
1200 W. Washington
Phoenix, AZ 85007-2929
Tel.: 602-542-3135
Tel.: 800-345-5819 (Arizona residents only)
or
400 W. Congress
Tucson, AZ 85701-1347
Tel.: 520-628-6560
Web site: www.cc.state.az.us/

What they supply:

State provides fill-in-the-blanks sets of Articles of Incorporation, both for corporations that propose tax exempt status and also for corporations that will be subject to taxation. They also provide a Certificate of Disclosure and a sample cover letter for filing your Articles.

What must be filed:

Complete your Articles and file the original and two copies. Also fill in the Certificate of Disclosure and attach it to your articles. Enclose the filing fee. After filing your Articles must be published within 60 days in a newspaper of general circulation in the county of the place of business in Arizona. There must be three consecutive publications of a copy of the approved articles. Within 90 days of filing an affidavit evidencing the publication must be filed with the Commission.

Name Requirements:

Check your corporate name with the Commission prior to filing your documents by calling (602) 542-3135 in Phoenix or (520) 628-6560 in Tucson. A name may be formally reserved for a $10 fee for 120 days.

Directors Requirements:

Your corporation must at least have three directors. The names and addresses of the initial directors must be entered in Article 9.

Articles requirements:

Enter one of the specific valid purposes for which a nonprofit corporation may be formed in Article 3.

In Article 5 and 6 you must enter the applicable Section number of of the IRS code under which your corporation plans to organize. Contact your local IRS office to obtain these numbers.

In Article 8 enter the name and business address of your initial statutory agent. This statutory agent has to sign the Articles on the bottom of the page.

Also complete your Certificate of Disclosure which has to be filed with your Articles. It contains information about your officers, directors and anyone involved in the corporation.

Filing fees:

$40, payable to the Arizona Corporation Division. For expedited service, add an extra $35.

Reports:

The annual report must be filed by April 15 (or by the 15th day of the 4th month of the corporation's fiscal year if a different fiscal year has been adopted).

Statute: Arizona Revised Statutes, Section 10-2300

TAXES:

Department of Revenue
Corporate Section
1200 W. Washington St.
Phoenix, AZ 85007
Tel.: 602-542-3935
Fax: 602-542-4111
Website: http://www.revenue.state.az.us/

Automatic Exemption: No

CHARITABLE SOLICITATION:

Secretary of State
1700 West Washington, 7th Floor
Phoenix, AZ 85007-2808
Tel.: 602-542-4286

Statute:

Arizona Revised Statutes, Sections 44-1522, 44-6551 et seq.

Exemption: first $25.000 or 10 or less donors

Annual filing: Yes

Accept URS: No

ARKANSAS

INCORPORATION:

Secretary of State
Corporation Division
State Capital, Room 58
Little Rock, AR 72201 - 1094
Tel.: 501-682-5151
Website: www.sosweb.state.ar.us

What they supply:

State provides two copies of fill-in-the-blanks Articles of Incorporation and a non-profit corporation filing fee schedule.

What must be filed:

Complete both copies of the fill-in-the-blanks articles and file them with the Secretary of State. Make sure that the articles are signed by all incorporators.

Name requirements:

The corporate name may not contain a word or phrase which indicates that it is organized for a purpose other than one or more of the purposes contained in your Articles of Incorporation. It has to contain "corporation," "incorporated," "company" or an abbreviation. Note: Name may not end in "company" if preceded by "and".

Director requirements:

Your corporation must have at least three directors. The directors don't have to be residents of Arkansas.

Article requirements:

The minimum requirements for your articles are as follows:

- the name of the corporation
- the determination whether the corporation shall be a public-benefit, a mutual-benefit or a religious corporation

- a statement whether or not the corporation will have members
- if applicable, provisions regarding the distribution of assets on dissolution
- the street address and the name of the corporation's initial registered office
- the address and signature of each incorporator

Filing fees:

$50, payable to the Secretary of State

Reports: Not required

Statute: Arkansas Code, Title 4, Sec. 28-206

TAXES:

Department of Finance and Administration
7th & Wolfe
P.O.Box 1272
Little Rock, AR 72203-0919
Tel.: 501-682-4779
Fax.: 501-682-7900
Website: http://www.state.ar.us/dfa

Automatic Exemption: No

CHARITABLE SOLICITATION:

Office of the Attorney General
Consumer Protection Division
200 Tower Building
323 Center Street
Little Rock, AR 72201
Tel.: 501-682-2007

Statute: Ark. Code Ann. 4-28-406

Exemption:

$10,000, provided all fundraising activities are carried out by volunteers.

Annual Filing: Yes

Accept URS: Yes

CALIFORNIA

INCORPORATION:

Office of the Secretary of State
Limited Liability Company Unit
1500 - 11th Street, 3rd Floor
P.O. Box 944228
Sacramento, CA 94244-2280
Tel.: 916-653-3795
Website: www.ss.ca.gov/

What they supply:

State provides sample Articles of Incorporation for religious, public benefit and mutual benefit nonprofits with instructions. They also provide a booklet with tax exemption application forms (form FTB 3500).

What must be filed:

Draft your own articles accordingly to the applicable sample articles provided by the state. The documents must be typed in black ink on one side of the paper only.

To avoid the initial annual franchise tax of $800 complete the application form for exemption from franchise tax (form 3500), enclose all attachments called for in the instructions and file this application together with the original and four copies of your articles. Also enclose the $25 application filing fee, the State filing fee and a self-addressed envelope. The Secretary of State will certify two copies without charge.

Name requirements:

The following words are not allowed in the corporation's name: bank, trust, trustee.

Director requirements:

Your nonprofit corporation must have at least one director. The directors don't have to be residents of California.

Articles requirement:

Your articles must have the following minimum contents:

- the corporate name
- the general purpose (Mutual Benefit Corporation, Public Benefit Corporation, Religious Corporation) <u>and</u> the specific purpose of the corporation

- name and California street address of the initial agent (post office box alone is not acceptable)
- signature and typed name (directly below the signature)of at least one incorporator
- if directors are stated in the articles, each named person must acknowledge and sign the articles
- special statements required to be included in the articles to get the tax exemption (only where applicable—please contact the Franchise Tax Board under the address typed below)

Filing fees:

$30, for expedited processing of documents, add a special handling fee of $15. The special handling fee must be remitted by a separate check and will be retained whether documents are filed or rejected.

Reports:

You have to file an annual report within 120 days of the end of corporation's fiscal year.

Statute:

California Code, Nonprofit Corporation Law, Public Benefit Corporations, Section 5122

TAXES:

Franchise Tax Board
9645 Butterfield Way
Sacramento, CA 95827
Tel.: 800-852-5711
Fax: 916-369-4505
Website: http://www.ftb.ca.gov

Automatic exemption: No

CHARITABLE SOLICITATION:

Registry of Charitable Trust
P.O.Box 903447
Sacramento, CA 94203-4470
Tel.: 916-445-2021

Statute:

California Government Code 12580-12596; California Code of Regulations, Title 11, 300-310, 999.1-999.4; Bus. & Prof. Code Sec. 17510-17510.85; 22930; California Corporation Code, Sec. 5223-5250

Exemption: $25,000

Annual filing: Yes

Accept URS: Yes

COLORADO

INCORPORATION:

Secretary of State
Corporations Office
1560 Broadway, Suite 200
Denver, CO 80202
Tel.: 303-894-2251
Fax: 303-894-2242
Website: www.state.co.us/gov_dir/sos/pubs.html

What they supply:

State sends you fill-in-the-blanks Articles of Incorporation with detailed instructions and information about how to apply for the tax exemption. They also provide information about the latest amendments concerning the non-profit statutes.

What must be filed:

Make a copy of the fill-in-the-blanks Articles and complete both documents by typing them in black ink. File both originals and enclose the filing fee.

Name requirements:

By law the corporate name may not include any word or phrase that implies a purpose not included in the Articles of Incorporation. But because the law doesn't require your articles to state a certain purpose, the Secretary of State will accept any name that is not deceptively similar to any other domestic corporation already on file with the Secretary of State.

It's not necessary to use a "corporate ending" (e.g. Corporation, Co. or Incorporated).

Directors requirements:

Your company must have at least one director and one officer. They don't have to be residents of Colorado.

Articles requirements:

The minimum requirements for a Colorado nonprofit corporation are as follows:

• the corporate name
• the name and street address of the corporation's registered agent and office

• the name and address of each incorporator
• a statement whether or not the corporation will have members
• provisions regarding distribution of assets upon dissolution
• the number of directors your corporation shall have

Make sure that each incorporator listed signs the articles.

Filing fees:

$50, payable to the Secretary of State

Reports:

You have to file reports every two years (between January 1 and May 1).

Statute:

Chapter 7–122 of the Colorado Revised Statutes, Colorado Nonprofit Corporation Act

TAXES:

Department of Revenue
Taxpayer Service Division
1375 Sherman St.
Denver, CO 80261
Tel.: 303-534-1208
Website: http://www.state.co.us/gov_dir/revenue_dir/home_rev.html

Automatic Exemption: Yes

CHARITABLE SOLICITATION:

Secretary of State
1560 Broadway, 2nd Floor
Denver, CO 80202
Tel.: 303-894-2200

Statute: Revised Statutes, Title 6, Article 16

Exemption:

None, but you must only register with a solicitation form. There are no specific requirements like annual fees etc.

Annual filing: By campaign—no renewal required

Accept URS: No

CONNECTICUT

INCORPORATION:

Secretary of State
30 Trinity Street
P.O. Box 150470
Hartford, CT 06106-0470
Tel.: 860-566-4128
Website: /www.state.ct.us/sots/

What they supply:

State provides all necessary fill-in-the-blanks forms with instructions such as the Certificate of Incorporation, an application for reservation of a name, a "First Report" form and a request form for expedited service. Also a fee schedule is provided.

What must be filed:

Type or print your Certificate of Incorporation in black ink. File only the original together with the filing fee.

Name requirements:

Your corporation name must include the words "corporation," "incorporated," or "company," or the abbreviation "corp.," "inc.," or "co." and must be distinguishable from other company names on file with the Secretary of State.

A name reservation can be made for a $30 fee for 120 days using the application form provided by the State.

Directors requirements:

Your corporation must have at least three directors. They don't have to be residents of Connecticut.

Articles requirements:

In Article 2 check the appropriate box whether your corporation shall have members and what rights they shall have. Enter the name and address of your registered agent in Article 3 and make sure the agent signs the Acceptance of appointment.

As a nonprofit, non stock corporation the purpose of your corporation may be "to engage in any lawful act or activity for which corporations may be formed under the Connecticut Revised Non stock corporation Act" (Article 4).

Filing fees:

$40 (includes a $30 statutory franchise tax), payable to the Connecticut Secretary of State.

Reports:

The Organization and First Report must be filed within 30 days of the date on which the corporation holds its organization meeting. The filing fee $25.

Statute:

Connecticut General Statutes, Nonstock Corporations, Sec. 33-427

TAXES:

Department of Revenue Services
92 Farmington Ave.
Hartford, CT 06105
Tel.: 203-566-8520
Fax: 203-297-5714
Website: http://www.state.ct.us/drs/

Automatic exemption: Yes

CHARITABLE SOLICITATION:

Attorney General
Public Charities Unit
55 Elm Street
Hartford, CT 06106
Tel.: 203-566-5836

Statute:

Connecticut General Statutes 21A-190A, et seq.

Exemption:

Less than $25,000 annually and not paying anyone primarily to raise funds.

Annual filing: Yes

Accept URS: Yes

DELAWARE

INCORPORATION:

State of Delaware
Division of Corporations
P.O.Box 898
Dover, DE 19903
Tel.: 302-739-3073
Name Reservation: Tel.: 900-420-8042
Website: www.state.de.us/corp

What they supply:

State provides complete booklet "Incorporate in Delaware" which contains any information about doing business in Delaware. The booklet includes fee schedules, a franchise tax schedule, phone and fax directory, a list of registered agents and fill-in-the-blanks forms for every kind of corporation.

What must be filed:

Complete the fill-in-the-blanks form Certificate of Incorporation for "non-stock corporations." Print or type your documents in black ink and submit any additional documents in the US letter size (8.5"x11"). File the original Certificate of Formation and one exact copy. Enclose the filing fee.

Name requirements:

Your corporate name must include one of the following words: "Association, Company, Corporation, Club, Foundation, Fund, Incorporated, Institute, Society, Union, Syndicate," or one of the abbreviations "Co., Corp., Inc."

A name reservation can be made by calling 900-420-8042. The name will be reserved for 30 days for a fee of $10.

Directors requirements:

Your corporation must have one or more directors. They don't have to be residents of Delaware.

Articles requirements:

Non-profit corporations must add "This Corporation shall be a nonprofit corporation" in the third Article.

In Article 4 you're asked to state your membership conditions but you can also leave that to be regulated by your By-laws.

Filing fees:

The filing fee for nonprofit corporations is $50 plus the appropriate county fee of $6.00 for administration and $9.00 per page with a two page minimum.

The fees are payable to the "Delaware Secretary of State" and can be made by check or credit card.

The Division of Corporations offers expedited service for additional fees:

- Priority 1 (completed within 2 hours of receipt when received by 7:00 pm E.S.T.): $ 500
- same day (when received by 2:00 pm): up to $200
- 24 hour (filing will be completed the next business day): up to $100

Reports:

The annual report has to be submitted to the Division of Corporations in November/ December each year. The filing for the annual report is $20.

Statute: DCA Title 8, Sec. 102

TAXES:

Department of Finance
Division of Revenue
Carvel Office Building
820 French St.
Wilmington, DE 19801
Tel.: 302-577-3315
Fax: 302-577-3106
Website: http://www.state.de.us/revenue

Automatic Exemption: No

CHARITABLE SOLICITATION:

Attorney General
Civil Division
The Wilmington Tower
Wilmington, DE 19899
Tel.: 302-577-2500

Statute: There is no statute, requiring registration.

Exemption:

No current registration requirements for solicitation of charitable contributions

Annual filing: No

Accept URS: No

DISTRICT OF COLUMBIA

INCORPORATION:

Department of Consumer and Regulatory Affairs
Corporation Division
941 North Capitol Street N.E.
Washington, D.C. 20002
Tel.: 202-727-7283
Website: www.dcra.org

What they supply:

State provides general guidelines to draft your own Articles of Incorporation and specific guidelines to form a non-profit corporation together with sample Articles. Also a filing fee schedule is provided. Note that the mailing address on the guidelines may be incorrect (especially if you use the guidelines from 1999 and before). The Department of Consumer and Regulatory Affairs has recently moved to a new location. The correct mailing, effective immediately, is given above.

What must be filed:

Draft your own Articles accordingly to the instructions and the sample articles given by the State. Use plain bond paper, either U.S. letter or legal size. Submit two originally signed and notarized sets of articles.

Name requirements:

The corporate name may not include language that implies the corporation is organized for purposes other than those stated in the Articles of Incorporation. The name may not be the same or similar to the name of a corporation registered under the law of D.C. and shall not indicate that corporation is organized under an act of Congress.

Directors requirements:

Your corporation must at least have three directors. They don't have to be residents of D.C.

Articles requirements:

The minimum requirements for your Articles are as follows:
- the name of your corporation
- the period of duration (this can be perpetual or a specific period)
- a specific purpose for which the corporation is organized

- a statement whether the corporation shall have members
- if your corporation shall have members, the number of classes of members and the different qualifications and rights of the members of each class
- the manner in which directors shall be elected or appointed and a statement, which class of members shall have the right to elect directors
- a provision of the regulation of the internal affairs of your corporation
- the name of your initial registered agent and the address of your initial registered office
- the number of initial directors your corporation shall have and their names and addresses
- the names and addresses of each incorporator (incorporators must be at least 21 years of age)

Filing fees:

$50, payable to the "D.C. Treasurer"

Reports:

You have to file an annual report by April 15.

Statute: D.C. Code, Title 29, Chapter 5

TAXES:

Department of Finance and Revenue
300 Indiana Ave. NW
Washington, DC 2001
Tel.: 202-727-6083
Fax: 202-727-6083
Website: http://www.dccfo.com

Automatic Exemption: No

CHARITABLE SOLICITATION

Dept. of Consumer & Regulatory Affairs
614 H Street, NW
Washington, DC 2001
Tel.: 202-727-7086

Statute: D.C. Code 2-711 (1981 ed.)

Exemption: less than $1,500 annually, provided all functions in the corporation are carried out by unpaid persons.

Annual filing: Yes

Accept URS: Yes

FLORIDA

INCORPORATION:

Secretary of State
Division of Corporations
P.O. Box 6327
Tallahassee, FL 32314
Tel.: 904-488-9000
Fax: 904-487-6052
Web site: www.dos.state.fl.us

What they supply:

State provides booklet " Division of Corporations Services Guide" with all important information and a copy of the Florida Not For Profit Corporation Act. They also include a Name Registration Packet and fill-in-the-blanks forms for a nonprofit corporation with specific instructions.

What must be filed:

Complete the sample articles and file the original and one copy. Also complete the transmittal letter provided by the state and attach it to your articles. Enclose the correct filing fee.

Name requirements:

Your corporation name must include one of the words "Corporation, Corp., Incorporated, or Inc." As a nonprofit corporation you must not use the words "Company" or "Co." Name availability can be checked by calling 904-488-9000 prior to filing your articles. You can reserve a name for a fee of $35 for a period of 120 days.

Directors requirements:

There must be at least three directors who must be 18 years of age or older but not need to be residents of Florida.

Articles requirements:

The minimum requirements for your articles are as follows:
- the name of your corporation
- the principal place of business and mailing address of the corporation

- a specific purpose for which your corporation is formed
- a statement, in which manner the directors are elected or appointed
- the name and Florida street address of your initial registered agent—make sure your registered agent signs the articles in the space on the bottom page
- the name and signature of each incorporator

Filing fees:

$70 (includes $35 filing fee and $35 for the Designation of the Registered Agent).
For an optional $ 52.50 you receive a Certified Copy. Make your checks payable to the Department of State.

Reports:

The annual report must be filed on or before May 1 each year. The filing fee is $ 61.25.

Statute: Chapter 617, Florida Statutes

TAXES:

Department of Revenue
The Carlton Building, #104
Tallahassee, FL 32399-0100
Tel.: 904-488-6800
Website: http://sun6.dms.state.fl.us/dor/

Automatic Exemption: No

CHARITABLE SOLICITATION:

Department of Agriculture
Division of Consumer Services
P.O.Box 6700
Tallahassee, FL 32314-6700
Tel.: 904-488-2221

Statute: Florida Statutes, Chapter 496

Exemption:

less than $25,000 carried out by unpaid fundraisers

Annual filing: Yes

Accept URS: No

GEORGIA

INCORPORATION:

Secretary of State
2 Martin Luther King, Jr. Drive
Suite 315, West Tower
Atlanta, GA 30330
Tel: 404 656-2817
Fax: 404-651-9059
Website: www.sos.state.ga.us

What they supply:

State provides sample Articles of Incorporation and instructions to draft your own articles. Attached is a fill-in-the-blanks "Transmittal Information" form which has to be filed with your articles.

What must be filed:

Draft your own articles accordingly to the guidelines given by the state. Submit the original and one exact copy. Also fill in the "Transmittal Information" form and attach it to your articles. Enclose the filing fee.

Note that all corporations have to publish a notice of intent to incorporate in the official legal newspaper of the county in which the registered office of the corporation is located (the Clerk of Superior Court will give you advice). You must forward your notice of intent together with a $40 publication fee directly to the newspaper on the next business day after filing your articles. A sample notice of incorporation is included in the instructions how to draft your articles.

Name requirements:

A corporate name can and should be reserved prior to filing. A reservation can be made by calling 404-656-2817 or at Corporations Divisions web site given above. You will receive a name reservation number that remains in effect for 90 days.

Directors requirements:

Your corporation must have at least 3 directors. They don't have to be residents of Georgia.

Articles requirements:

Your articles must contain the following minimum:

- the name of the corporation

- a statement, that the corporation is organized pursuant to the Georgia Nonprofit Corporation Code
- the name of the registered agent and the street address of its office in Georgia (a post office box address alone is not acceptable)
- the name and address of each incorporator
- a statement whether the corporation shall have members
- the mailing address of the corporation
- a signature of one of the incorporators named in the articles

Filing fees:

$60, payable to the Secretary of State

Reports:

You have to file an annual report between January 1 and April 1.

Statute: GCA, Title 14-2-120, Sec. 2702

TAXES:

Department of Revenue
Tax Exemption
P.O. Box 38467
Atlanta, GA 30334
Tel.: 404-656-7043
Website:
http://www2.state.ga.us/Departments/DOR/

Automatic Exemption: No

CHARITABLE SOLICITATION:

Secretary of State
Business Services & Regulation
2 Martin Luther King Drive
Suite 802 - West Tower
Atlanta, GA 30334
Tel.: 404-656-4910

Statute: O.C.G.A. 43-17-1, et seq.

Exemption: less than $25,000 annually

Annual Filing: Yes

Accept URS: Yes

HAWAII

INCORPORATION:

Business Registration Division
Department of Commerce and Consumer Affairs
1010 Richards Street
P.O. Box 541
Honolulu, HI 96809
Tel.: 808-586-2727
Website: www.state.hi.us/dcca/dcca.html

What they supply:

State provides fill-in-the-blanks Articles of Incorporation in duplicate, but no instructions are given how to complete them.

What must be filed:

Complete both copies and file them with the Secretary of State. Enclose the filing fee.

Name requirements:

The corporate name may not include language that implies the corporation is organized for purposes other than those stated in the Articles of Incorporation. The name may not be the same or similar to the name of a corporation registered under the law of Hawaii, unless with written consent of the registered name holder, and with added words to distinguish the names.

Directors requirements:

Your corporation must at least have three members and also at least one president, one vice-president, one secretary and one treasurer.

Articles requirements:

Your articles shall set forth the following minimum:

- the name of your corporation
- the address of the corporation's office
- the purpose for which the corporation is organized
- the names and street addresses of the initial directors
- the names and street addresses of the initial officer

- a statement whether the corporation shall have members
- the signature of each incorporator

Filing fees:

$50, payable to the "Department of Commerce and Consumer Affairs," for an extra $50 you get expedited service (filing will be done within five business days, otherwise at least 20 business days).

Reports:

You have to file an annual report between January 1 and March 31.

Statute:

Title 23, Section 415B- 34, Hawaii Revised Statutes

TAXES:

Department of Taxation
Keelikalani Building
830 Punchbowl St.
P.O. Box 259
Honolulu, HI 96809
Tel.: 808-587-1510
Fax: 808-587-1633
Website: http://www.state.hi.us/tax/tax.html

Automatic Exemption: Yes

CHARITABLE SOLICITATION:

Dept. of Commerce and Consumer Affairs
P.O. Box 40
Honolulu, HI 96810
Tel.: 808-586-2727

Statute:

Hawaii Statutes, Chapter 467B (Solicitation of Funds from the Public)

Exemption:

No current registration requirements for solicitation of charitable contributions.

Annual filing: No

Accept URS: No

IDAHO

INCORPORATION:

Secretary of State
700 W. Jefferson, Basement West
Boise, ID 83720-0080
Tel.: 208-334-2301
Website: www.idsos.state.id.us/

What they supply:

The State only sends you a copy of the Nonprofit Corporation Act, but no forms of Articles of Incorporation. You have to draft your own articles accordingly to the legal requirements shown in Section 30-3-17 of the Act.

What must be filed:

Your self drafted documents must be typewritten or printed and executed either by an officer (if there's such), an incorporator. or a fiduciary. File the original and one exact copy together with the filing fee.

Name requirements:

Your company name must contain the words "corporation, company, incorporated, or limited" or an abbreviation of these words.

You can reserve a name by filing an application with the Secretary of State. If the name is available it will be reserved for a period of four months for a fee of $20.

Directors requirements:

Your corporation must have at least three directors, but if your corporation is going to be a *religious* corporation your board of directors needs only one person.

Articles requirements:

Your articles must contain the following minimum requirements:

- the name of the corporation
- the purpose for which the corporation is formed, this can be to transact any and all lawful activity for which a nonprofit corporation can be formed
- the names and addresses of your initial directors
- the name of your initial registered agent and the address of his registered office
- the name and address of each incorporator

- a statement whether or not the corporation shall have members
- any other provision regarding the distribution of assets on dissolution

Make sure that each incorporator signs the articles.

Filing fees:

$30, payable to the "Secretary of State"

Reports:

The first annual report must be delivered to the Secretary of State between July 1 and November 1 of the year following the calendar year in which the corporation was incorporated. The subsequent annual reports must be delivered between July 1 and November 1 each year.. The form for the annual report is furnished by the Secretary of State.

There's no fee for filing the annual report !

Statute:

Title 30, Chapter 3 of the Idaho Statutes (Idaho Nonprofit Corporation Act)

TAXES:

State Tax Commission
Department of Revenue and Taxation
800 Park Blvd.
Boise, ID 83772
Tel.: 208-334-7660
Website: http://www.state.id.us/tax/

Automatic Exemption: Yes

CHARITABLE SOLICITATION:

Attorney General
Business Regulation Division
Statehouse, Room 210
Boise, ID 83720
Tel.: 208-334-2400

Statute:

Idaho Statutes, Title 48, Chapter 10 and 12 (Charitable Solicitation Act, Telephone Solicitation Act)

Exemption:

No current registration requirements for solicitation of charitable contributions

Annual filing: No

Accept URS: No

ILLINOIS

INCORPORATION:

> Secretary of State
> Business Services Dept.
> 328 Howlett Building, Room 359
> Springfield, IL 62756
> Tel.: 217-782-9523 (general information)
> Tel.: 217-782-9520 (Name availability)
> Website: www.sos.state.il.us

What they supply:

State provides fill-in-the-blanks Articles of Incorporation in duplicate and a booklet containing information how to file your articles.

What must be filed:

Type or print your documents in black ink and file the original and one exact copy. Enclose the filing fee.

After you receive the certificate and your file stamped articles from the Secretary of State, you must file them with the office of the Recorder of Deeds of the county in which your registered office is located. The recording must be within 15 days after receiving your certificate.

Name requirements:

Your corporate name may not contain words regarding any political party. It must be distinguishable from any other Illinois corporation on file with the Secretary of State. Select a name that does not indicate that your corporation is a corporation for profit.

For name availability call 217-782-9520 prior to filing, a name reservation can be made by a written request listing the name wanted and a brief description of the corporate purpose, the fee is $25.

Directors requirements:

Your company must at least have three directors, who do not have to be residents or corporation members.

Articles requirements:

The purpose for which your corporation is formed (Article 4) must be a specific purpose and may not be too general or broad. A list of allowable purposes can be found in the booklet provided by the state (see page 3 of the booklet). Also in Article 4 check the appropriate box whether your corporation shall be a Condominium Association or whether your corporation shall be Cooperative Housing or Homeowner's Association.

Filing fees:

$50, payable to the Secretary of State.

Reports:

The annual report is due before the first day of the corporation's anniversary month each year. The forms will be sent to your registered agent approximately 60 days before the due date.

Statute:

Chapter 805 Act 105, Illinois Compiled Statutes 1992, "The General Not For Profit Corporation Act of 1986"

TAXES:

> Illinois Department of Revenue
> Income Tax Division
> 101 W. Jefferson St.
> Springfield, IL 92794
> Tel.: 217-782-9922
> or
> 100 West Randolph
> Concourse 300
> Chicago, IL 60601
> Tel.: 312-917-3222
> Website: http://www.revenue.state.il.us/

Automatic Exemption: Yes

CHARITABLE SOLICITATION:

> Attorney General
> Charitable Trust Division
> 100 West Randolph, 12th Floor
> Chicago, IL 60601-3175
> Tel.: 312-814-2595

Statute: 760 ILCS 55/1; 225 ILCS 460/1

Exemption:

Corporations with gross revenue less than $15,000 and unpaid fundraisers are required to register but are exempt from annual financial filing.

Annual filing: Yes

Accept URS: Yes

INDIANA

INCORPORATION:

Secretary of State
Room 155, State House
302 W. Washington, Room E018
Indianapolis, IN 46204
Tel.: 317-232-6576 or
Tel.: 317-232-6531 or
Tel.: 800-726-8000
Website: www.state.in.us/sos

What they supply:

State provides three copies of fill-in-the-blanks Articles of Incorporation and a booklet "Business Owner's Guide to State Government" which contains general information how to conduct business in Indiana.

What must be filed:

Type or print all three copies of the fill-in-the-blanks forms and file them with the Secretary of State. Enclose the filing fee.

Name requirements:

Your corporate name must include one of the words "Corporation, Incorporated, Limited, or Company" or any abbreviation of these words.

Directors requirements:

Your corporation must have at least 3 directors. They don't have to be residents of Indiana.

Article requirements:

In Article 3 check the appropriate box whether your corporation is a public benefit, a religious or a mutual benefit corporation. Also check in Article 5 whether your corporation will have members. Make sure that your articles are signed by each incorporator.

Filing fees:

$30, payable to the Secretary of State

Reports:

Nonprofit corporations have to file annual reports with a $10 filing fee.

Statute:

Indiana Code 23-17, Indiana Nonprofit Corporation Act of 1991

TAXES:

Department of Revenue
N 248 Indiana Government Center N
100 Senate Ave.
Indianapolis, IN 46204-2253
Tel.: 317-232-2188
Website: http://www.ai.org/dor/index.html

Automatic Exemption: No

CHARITABLE SOLICITATION:

Attorney General
Consumer Protection Division
Indiana Government Center South
402 W. Washington St, 5th Floor
Indianapolis, IN 46204-2770
Tel.: 317-232-6201

Statute: Indiana Code 23-7, Chapter 8

Exemption:

No current registration requirements for solicitations of charitable contributions

Annual Filing: No

Accept URS: No

IOWA

INCORPORATION:

Secretary of State
Corporations Division
Hoover Building
Des Moines, IA 50319
Tel.: 515-281-5204
Fax: 515-242-6556
Website: www.sos.state.ia.us/

What they supply:

State provides guidelines how to draft your own articles and a short summary of the Iowa Nonprofit Corporation Act.

What must be filed:

Draft your own Articles of Incorporation accordingly to the guidelines and Section 504A.29 of the Nonprofit Corporation Act. See "Articles Requirements" below for details. Deliver the original document and one exact copy together with the filing fee.

Name requirements:

The corporate name may not include language that implies the corporation is organized for purposes other than those stated in the Articles of Incorporation. The name may not be the same or similar to the name of a corporation registered under the law of Iowa.

Directors requirements:

Your corporation must have at least 1 director who doesn't have to be a resident of Iowa.

Article requirements:

Your articles must include the following minimum:
- the name of the corporation and the Chapter of the Code under which incorporated
- if you want your corporation to be formed for a limited time the period of duration, skip that if it shall be perpetual
- the purpose for which the organization is organized (must be a charitable, literary, educational or scientific purpose)
- any provisions which set forth the regulation of the internal affairs of the corporation, including provisions of the distribution of assets upon dissolution
- the name of the registered agent and the address of the initial registered office
- the number and the names and addresses of the initial directors
- if applicable, any provision limiting any of the corporate powers
- the date on which the corporate existence shall begin (not more than ninety days in the future)—you can skip this, your corporation will then exist from the date the state issues the certificate of incorporation
- the name and address of each incorporator

Make sure that the person executing the documents signs and states his name and capacity in which he/she signs.

Filing fees:

$20, payable to the secretary of state

Reports:

You have to file an annual report between January 1 and March 31.

Statutes: Iowa Code, 504A.29

TAXES:

Iowa Department of Revenue
Business Section
Hoover Office Building
Des Moines, IA 50319
Tel.: 515-281-3114
Fax: 515-242-6040
Website:
http://www.state.ia.us/government/drf/index.html

Automatic Exemption: No

CHARITABLE SOLICITATION:

Attorney General
Consumer Protection Division
1300 East Walnut
Hoover State Building
Des Moines, IA 50319
Tel.: 515-281-5926

Statute: Code of Iowa, Chapter 13C

Exemption:

No current registration requirements for solicitation of charitable contributions.

Annual filing: No

Accept URS: No

KANSAS

INCORPORATION:

Secretary of State
Corporation Division
State Capitol, 2nd Floor 300 SW 10th St.
Topeka, KS 66612-1594
Tel.: 913-296- 4593
Website: www.kssos.org

What they supply:

State provides fill-in-the-blanks Articles of Incorporation with filing instructions.

What must be filed:

Complete the fill-in-the-blanks form and file the original and one exact copy. Note that the Articles of Incorporation must be notarized. Enclose the filing fee.

Name requirements:

Your corporation's name must include one of the following words indicating a corporation "Incorporated, Inc., Association, Church, Club, Foundation, Fund, Institute or Society." It must be different from any corporation's name already existing in Kansas.

Directors requirements:

Your corporation must have at least three directors. They don't have to be residents of Kansas.

Articles requirements:

The purpose your corporation is formed for must be stated in Article 3, a general statement that the purpose is to "engage in any lawful act or activity for which nonprofit corporations may be organized under the Kansas General Corporation Code" is sufficient. You should check with the IRS prior to filing whether your purpose must be specific one.

If you want to apply for the federal tax exempt status you must check the "No" box in Article 4 to make clear that your corporation won't issue capital stock.

Enter the names and mailing addresses of the persons serving as initial directors until the first annual meeting. Make sure the incorporator (minimum of one) signs the articles.

Filing fees:

$20, payable to the Secretary of State

Reports:

Your corporation must file an annual report with an annual privilege fee (ask Secretary of State for actual fee). The report form will be send to the registered office prior to the due date. The first report will not be required until your corporation is at least six months old.

Statute: KSA, Corporations, 17-6002

TAXES:

Kansas Department of Revenue
Docking State Office Building
915 S.W. Harrison St.
Topeka, KS 66612-1588
Tel.: 913-296-6661
Fax: 913-296-7928
Website: http://www.ink.org/public/kdor/

Automatic Exemption: Yes

CHARITABLE SOLICITATION:

Secretary of State
Corporate Division
Capitol Building, 2nd Floor
Topeka, KS 66612
Tel.: 913-296-2236

Statute: KSA 17-1760 et seq.

Exemption: $10,000

Annual filing: Yes

Accept URS: Yes

KENTUCKY

INCORPORATION:

Commonwealth of Kentucky
Office of the Secretary of State
P.O.Box 718
Frankfort, KY 40602
Tel.: 502-564-2848
Fax: 502-564-7330
Website: www.sos.state.ky.us

What they supply:

State provides guidelines how to draft your own Articles of Incorporation and general information about corporations.

What must be filed:

Your articles must be typewritten or printed and signed by an incorporator if no director has been selected. File the original and two exact copies of your articles and enclose the correct filing fee.

The Secretary of State will return two "filed" stamped copies to your registered agent's office.

Name requirements:

The corporation name must include the words "corporation" or "incorporated" or the abbreviation "Inc." You can also use the word "company" or the abbreviation "Co." which must not be preceded by the word "and" or the abbreviation "&."

Check the name availability prior to filing by calling 502-564-2848. A name reservation can be made for a fee of $15 for a period of 120 days.

Directors requirements:

A Kentucky nonprofit corporation must have at least three directors.

Articles requirements:

The minimum requirements for your articles are as follows:

- the corporate name
- the purpose or purposes for which your corporation is organized
- the name of your initial registered agent and the address of its office

- the mailing address of the corporation's principal office
- the number of your initial directors and the names and mailing addresses of these persons
- the name and mailing address of each incorporator
- any provisions for distribution of assets on dissolution or final liquidation of your corporation

Filing fees:

$8 (eight !), payable to the Secretary of State

Reports:

You have to file an annual report each June.

Statute:

Kentucky Revised Statutes, Chapter 273

TAXES:

Commonwealth of Kentucky
Revenue Cabinet
Corporation Income Tax Section
Capitol Annex Building
Frankfort, KY 40620
Tel.: 502-564-3658
Website:
http://www.state.ky.us/agencies/revenue/revhome.htm

Automatic Exemption: No

CHARITABLE SOLICITATION:

Attorney General
Division of Consumer Protection
P.O. Box 2000
Frankfort, KY 40602-2000
Tel.: 502-573-2200

Statute: Kentucky Revised Statutes 367.650

Exemption: None

Annual filing: Yes

Accept URS: Yes

LOUISIANA

INCORPORATION:

Secretary of State
Corporations Division
P.O. Box 94125
Baton Rouge, LA 70804-9125
Tel.: 504-925-4704
Website: www.sec.state.la.us/

What they supply:

State provides single fill-in-the-blanks Articles of Incorporation with brief instructions.

What must be filed:

To obtain a federal tax identification number call the IRS at 901-546-3920 prior to filing your Articles. Complete the fill-in-the-blanks form provided by the state. Make sure that your registered agent signs the affidavit on the bottom of the second page. Both articles and affidavit have to be notarized. File only the original and enclose the filing fee.

Within 30 days after filing your Articles, a multiple original or a copy certified by the Secretary of State and a copy of the Certificate of Incorporation must be filed with the office of the recorder of mortgages in the parish where the corporation's registered office is located.

Name requirements

The name may not be the same or similar to the name of a corporation registered under the law of Louisiana, unless the corporation has failed to do business for two years or to pay franchise taxes for five years. The name may not imply the corporation is an administrative agency and shall not include the following words and phrases: assurance, bank, building and loan, casualty, cooperative, deposit, fiduciary, guarantee, homestead, indemnity, insurance, mutual, savings, security, surety, or trust.

Directors requirements:

Your corporation must have at least three directors. State the term of office of each director in Article 8.

Articles requirements:

In Article 2 check the first box if you don't want the purpose of your corporation to be limited.

If you want to apply for the federal tax-exempt status you must check "Non-stock basis" in Article 9 to make clear that your corporation doesn't issue stock. You then have to fill in Article 10 b, characterizing the qualifications which must be met to be a member of your corporation.

Filing fees:

$60, payable to the Secretary of State

Reports:

You have to file an annual report by May 15.

Statute:

Louisiana Revised Statutes, Chapter 12:203

TAXES:

Department of Revenue and Taxation
330 Ardenwood Drive
P.O. Box 201
Baton Rouge, LA 70821
Tel.: 504-925-4611
Website: http://www.rev.state.la.us/

Automatic Exemption: Yes

CHARITABLE SOLICITATION:

Attorney General
Consumer Protection Division
P.O. Box: 94005
Baton Rouge, LA 70804
Tel.: 504-342-9638

Statute: Louisiana Revised.Statutes. 51:1901-1904

Exemption: None

Annual filing: Yes

Accept URS: Yes

MAINE

INCORPORATION:

Secretary of State
Bureau of Corporations, Elections,
and Commissions
101 State House Station
Augusta, ME 04333-0101
Tel.: 207-287-4195 - form
Tel.: 800-872-3838 - business answers
Fax: 207-287-5874
Website: www.state.me.us/sos/sos.htm

What they supply:

State provides all fill-in-the-blanks forms required to incorporate, including Articles of Incorporation, a name application form and an acceptance form for the appointment of the registered agent. Also guidelines how to complete your Articles are provided.

What must be filed:

Type or print your articles in black ink. Make sure all your documents are dated by month, day and year and all bear original signatures. File the original and attach the completed Acceptance of Appointment as registered agent. Make sure to enclose the correct filing fee.

Name requirements:

You can reserve a corporate name prior to filing by submitting the Application for Reservation of Name form. If available, the name will be reserved for 120 days for a fee of $5.

Directors requirements:

Your corporation must have at least three directors. They do not have to be residents of Maine and there are no age restrictions.

Articles requirements:

If you don't want the purpose for which your corporation is formed to be limited just leave Article 2 blank, so your corporation is organized for all purposes permitted under the law.

Enter the number of your initial directors and of the directors to be elected on your first meeting in Article 4 and check the appropriate box in Article 5, whether or not your corporation shall have members.

Articles 6 and 7 are optional, check with the IRS prior to filing your articles, if your corporation has to meet the requirements stated in Article 7.

Filing fees:

$20, payable to the Deputy Secretary of State.

Reports:

Your annual report must be filed no later than June 1 the year following the year of incorporation. Use the Annual Report form issued by the Secretary of State.

Statute: Title 13-B, MRSA

TAXES:

Department of Finance and Administration
Bureau of Taxation
State House Station #24
Augusta, ME 04333
Tel.: 207-287-2086
Fax: 207-287-4028
Website:
http://janus.state.me.us/revenue/homepage.htm

Automatic Exemption: No

CHARITABLE SOLICITATION:

Financial Regulation
State House Station #35
Augusta, ME 04333
Tel.: 207-582-8723

Statute:

9 Maine Revised Statutes Annotated, Sec. 5001-5016

Exemption: $10,000 or 10 or less donors

Annual filing: Yes

Accept URS: Yes

MARYLAND

INCORPORATION:

State Department of Assessments and Taxation
Corporate Charter Division
301 West Preston Street, Rm. 809
Baltimore, MD 21201
Tel.: 410-225-1340
or
Tel.: 410-767-1330
Website: www.dat.state.md.us

What they supply:

The State sends out two different copies of fill-in-the-blanks Articles of Incorporation with guidelines how to draft them. One copy is for regular non-stock corporations, the other one for tax-exempt non stock corporations.

What must be filed:

Your documents must be typed. File only the original and enclose the filing fee.

Name requirements:

Your corporate name must contain the words "Corporation," "Incorporated," "Limited," "Inc.," "Corp.," or "Ltd." It must be distinguishable from any other corporate name already on file with the Secretary of State.

For name availability, call Tel.: 410-767-1330 prior to filing.

Directors requirements:

Your corporation must have at least one director. The director does not have to be a resident of Maryland.

Articles requirements:

Characterize the purpose for which your corporation is formed with one or two sentences in Article 3and make sure the purpose is charitable, religious, educational, or scientific.

Enter the minimum and maximum number of directors your corporation shall have and give the name and address of the initial director(s) in the space below.

Filing fees:

$40, payable to the Department of Assessments and Taxation.

Reports:

You have to file an annual report by April 15.

Statute:

Annotated Code of Maryland, Corporations and Associations, Sec. 2-104

TAXES:

Comptroller of the Treasury
Income Tax Division
P.O. Box 466
Annapolis, MD 21404-0446
Tel.: 401-974-3801
Website: http://www.comp.state.md.us

Automatic Exemption: No

CHARITABLE SOLICITATION:

Office of Secretary of State
Charitable Organization Division
State House
Annapolis, MD 21401
Tel.: 4110-974-5534

Statute:

Annotated Code of Maryland, Bus. Reg. Act., Sec. 6-101, et seq.

Exemption: $25,000

Annual filing: Yes

Accept URS: Yes

MASSACHUSETTS

INCORPORATION:

Secretary of State
Corporations Division
One Ashburton Place
17th Floor
Boston, MA 02108
Tel.: 617-727-9640
        or
Tel.: 617-727-9440
        or
Citizen Information Service
Tel.: 800-392-6090
Website: www.state.ma.us/massgov.htm

What they supply:

State provides sample Articles of Organization and a booklet "Organizing a Non-Profit Corporation" which contains all the information you need to draft your articles.

What must be filed:

Complete the sample articles and file the original document with the Secretary of State.

Name requirements:

Your corporate name must include the words "Limited," "Incorporated," or "Corporation" or abbreviations of these words. Religious organizations are exempt from this requirement.

For name availability call 617-727-9640. You can reserve a name prior to filing either by submitting a written application to the Secretary of State or in person. The name will be reserved for 30 days for a fee of $15. The reservation can be renewed once for another $15.

Directors requirements:

Your corporation must have at least 3 directors. They don't have to be residents of Massachusetts.

Articles requirements:

The purpose your corporation is formed for can be explained in simple language in Article 2, but if you want to apply for the tax-exempt status, characterize that purpose more specifically in Article 4. You should check with the IRS what requirements must be met to receive the tax-exemption.

Filing fees:

$35, payable to the "Commonwealth of Massachusetts."

Reports:

The annual report is due before November 1 each year.

Statute:

Chapter 180 of the Massachusetts General Laws

TAXES:

Department of Revenue
Customer Service Bureau
100 Cambridge St., 2nd Floor
Boston, MA 02204
Tel.: 617-887-6367
Tel.: 1-800-392-6089 (Toll-free in MA)
Website: http://www.state.ma.us/dor

Automatic Exemption: No

CHARITABLE SOLICITATION:

Attorney General
Division of Public Charities
One Ashburton Place
Boston, MA 02108
Tel.: 617-727-2200

Statute:

Massachusetts General Laws, Chapters 12 & 68

Exemption: $5,000 or 10 or less donors

Annual Filing: Yes

Accept URS: Yes

MICHIGAN

INCORPORATION:

Michigan Department of Commerce
Corporation and Securities Bureau,
Corporation Division
P.O. Box 30054
Lansing, MI 48909-7554
Tel.: 517-334-6302
Website: www.cis.state.mi.us/corp/

What they supply:

State provides fill-in-the-blanks Articles of Incorporation with filing instructions.

What must be filed:

Complete the fill-in-the-blanks form by typing or printing legibly in black ink. File only the original document together with the correct filing fee.

Name requirements:

The corporate name may not include language that implies the corporation is organized for purposes other than those stated in the Articles of Incorporation. The name may not be the same or similar to the name of a corporation registered under the law of Michigan, unless the name holder's written consent.

Directors requirements:

Your corporation must have at least one director. He does not have to be a resident of Michigan. There are no age restrictions for the directors.

Articles requirements:

Characterize the purpose for which your corporation is formed. This purpose must be specific, a general statement is not sufficient.

Complete either Article III (2) or III (3) depending on whether or not your corporation will issue stock. If you want to apply for the federal tax-exempt status your corporation will be on a non stock basis.

Note that except for educational corporations, which must have at least three incorporators, your corporation must only have one incorporator.

Filing fees:

$20, payable to the State of Michigan.

Reports:

You have to file an annually report by October 1. Note that the report must include any distribution of funds to shareholders or members and the amount of loans made to those persons and representatives of your corporation (directors, officers etc.).

Statutes:

Michigan Compiled Laws, MSA 21.197/202

TAXES:

Department of Treasury
Bureau of Collections
Treasury Building
Lansing, MI 48922
Tel.: 517-373-8030
Website: http://www.treas.state.mi.us

Automatic Exemption: Yes

CHARITABLE SOLICITATIONS:

Attorney General
Charitable Trust Section
P.O. Box 30214
Lansing, MI 48909
Tel.: 517-373-1152

Statute: MCLA 400.271

Exemption:

$25,000, provided nobody is paid to fundraise and the financial statements of your corporation are available to the public.

Annual filing: Yes

Accept URS: Yes

MINNESOTA

INCORPORATION:

Secretary of State
Division of Corporations
180 State Office Building
100 Constitution Ave.
St. Paul, MN 55155
Tel.: 612-296-2803
Website: www.sos.state.mn.us/bus.html

What they supply:

State provides sample form of Articles of Incorporation with guidelines how to complete each Article. The sample form includes only the minimum and it is not required that you use exactly this form. You can also draft your own articles, which must include these requirements.

What must be filed:

Print or type your document(s) legibly in black ink. File only the original.

Name requirements:

Corporate name has to be distinguishable from names of other corporations under the law of Minnesota. Nonprofit corporations can use words indicating that they are incorporated (e.g. "Incorporated," "Corp.," "Corporation," or "Company") but they are not required to use these words.

Directors requirements:

Your corporation must have at least three directors. They don't have to be residents of Minnesota.

Articles requirements:

Check the "Nonprofit Corporation" box at the top of your articles. Enter the name of your initial registered agent and the address of its registered office in Article 2.

Make sure that each incorporator (minimum of one) signs the articles.

Filing fees:

$70, payable to the Secretary of State.

Reports:

The state provides a form, which must be filed during the year.

Statute:

Minnesota Statutes Annotated 317A.111

TAXES:

Minnesota Department of Revenue
10 River Park Plaza
St. Paul, MN 55146
Tel.: 612-296-0555
Website: http://www.taxes.state.mn.us/

Automatic Exemption: No

CHARITABLE SOLICITATION:

Attorney General
Charities Division
NCL Tower, #1200
445 Minnesota Street
St. Paul, MN 55101-2131
Tel.: 612-296-6172

Statute: Minnesota Statutes, Chapter 309

Exemption: $25,000 annually, provided nobody is paid to fundraise.

Annual filing: Yes

Accept URS: Yes

MISSISSIPPI

INCORPORATION:

Secretary of State
Business Services Division
P.O. Box 136
Jackson, MS 39205-0136
Tel: 601-359-1333
Fax: 601-359-1499
      or
Tel.:800-256-3494
Website: www.sos.state.ms.us/

What they supply:

State provides computer-readable fill-in-the-blanks forms with detailed instructions how to meet the special requirements for computer-readability. Also a fill-in-the-name statement that the corporation is exclusively organized for religious, charitable, scientific, literary and educational purposes is provided.

What must be filed:

Complete the fill-in-the-blanks form exactly as described in the instructions. File only the original and enclose the filing fee. Attach the completed statement that your corporation is organized only for the purposes that will be recognized for the tax exemption.

Name requirements:

Nonprofit corporation names don't have to include words indicating their corporation status, but they may include such words, e.g. "Corporation," "Incorporated," "Inc.," or "Corp."

Directors requirements:

The number of directors is not specified in the Statutes. You can fix the number of directors in your corporation's articles or bylaws. The directors don't have to be residents of Mississippi.

Articles requirements:

In Article 4 nonprofit corporations can determine the period of duration, enter either a certain number of years or check " perpetual."
Give the name and address of each incorporator in Article 7.

Filing fees:

$50, payable to the Secretary of State.

Reports:

There is no duty to file an annual report. Rather the secretary of state requests an information report.

Statute:

Section 79-11-137 of the Mississippi Code of 1972

TAXES:

Mississippi State Tax Commission
Income and Franch Tax Division
P.O. Box 1033
Jackson, MS 39125
Tel.: 601-359-1141
Website: http://www.mstc.state.ms.us/

Automatic Exemption: Yes

CHARITABLE SOLICITATION

Secretary of State
P.O. Box 136
Jackson, MS 39205-0136
Tel.: 601-359-6357

Statute:

Mississippi Code Annotated Sec. 79-11-501, et seq.

Exemption:

$4000, provided no one is paid to fundraise.

Annual Filing: Yes

Accept URS: Yes

MISSOURI

INCORPORATION:

Secretary of State, Corporation Division
P.O. Box 778
Jefferson City, MO 65102
Tel.: 573-751-2359
Fax: 573-751-4153
Website: mosl.sos.state.mo.us/bus-ser/soscor.html

What they supply:

State provides two copies of fill-in-the-blanks Articles of Incorporation with general instructions and with special instructions what requirements have to be met to come within the purview of the federal tax exemption. They also include a fee schedule.

What must be filed:

Complete the fill-in-the-blanks forms and file your Articles in duplicate, make sure both documents are originally signed. Enclose the filing fee.

Name requirements:

Your corporate name must be distinguishable from any other company/corporation name already on record with the Secretary of State.

Directors requirements

Your corporation must have at least one president and/or chairman, one secretary, and one treasurer.

Articles requirements:

If you want to apply for the tax exempt status, make sure to meet the special requirements listed in the separate instructions. These requirements are as follows:

- the purpose for which your corporation is formed (Article 8) must be a charitable, educational, religious, or scientific one. To meet the State's requirements you also have to indicate exactly what your corporation is doing.

- the net income of your corporation may not distributed to the member, directors or other private persons except for reasonable compensation for services rendered

- your corporation may not take part in any political or legislative activities

- upon the dissolution of your corporation the remaining assets must be distributed either for the corporation's purposes or to any other similar corporation qualified as exempt organizations

Filing fees:

$25, payable to the "Director of Revenue"

Reports:

Your annual report, listing the officers and directors of the corporation, is due by August 31st each year but not in the first year of existence. The corporation will not remain in good standing if the report is not filed by November 30th.

Statute:

Missouri Revised Statutes, Chapter 347

TAXES:

Missouri Department of Revenue
Income Tax Bureau
P.O. Box 700
Jefferson City, MO 65105-0700
Tel.: 314-751-4541
Website: http://www.dor.state.mo.us/

Automatic Exemption: Yes

CHARITABLE SOLICITATION:

Attorney General
211 W. High Street
Jefferson, MO 65101
Tel.: 314-751-3321

Statute:

Missouri Revised Statutes, Sec. 407.450, et seq.

Exemption: None

Annual filing: Yes

Accept URS: Yes

MONTANA

INCORPORATION:

Secretary of State
P.O. Box 202801
Helena, MT 59620-2801
Tel.: 406-444-2034
Fax: 406-444-3976
Website: www.mt.gov/sos/index.htm

What they supply:

State provides all necessary fill-in-the-blanks forms with instructions such as the Certificate of Incorporation, an application for reservation of a name and for changing corporate name. Also a fee schedule and a booklet with general information are provided. The state offers "priority filing" (within 24 hours) for an additional fee of $20.

What must be filed:

First you have to check if the chosen name of your corporation is available. For this information you have to call the office of the Secretary of State. Than file the fill-in-the-blanks Articles and make a copy of the completed Articles. Mail both documents to the Secretary of State and enclose the filing fee.

Name requirements:

The name may not include language that implies the corporation is created for purposes other than stated in the Articles. It may not be the same or deceptively similar to the name of a corporation under the law of Montana. Last the name may not be fictitiously.

Directors requirements:

Your corporation must have at least 3 directors. They don't have to be residents of Montana

Articles requirements:

Your Articles have to include at least following contents:

- corporate name
- name and address of the registered agent and office in Montana
- name and address of each incorporator

- the specific purpose of the corporation (because the Internal Revenue Service requires specific language in order to qualify for nonprofit tax status it is advised that you contact the IRS)
- a statement whether the corporation will have members
- distribution of assets in the case of dissolution

Filing fees: $20, payable to the Secretary of State

Reports:

You have to file an annual report to April 15.

Statute: Revised Statutes of Montana 35-2-202

TAXES:

Department of Revenue
Income and Miscellaneous Tax Division
P.O. Box 5835
Helena, MT 59620-2701
Tel.: 406-444-3388
Fax: 406-444-1505
Website:
http://www.state.mt.us/revenue/index.htm

Automatic Exemption: No

CHARITABLE SOLICITATION:

Secretary of State
Room 225
Capitol Station
Helena, MT 59620
Tel.: 406-444-3665

Statute: Revised Statutes of Montana 35-2-118

Exemption:

No current registration requirements for solicitation of charitable contributions

Annual filing: No

Accept URS: No

NEBRASKA

INCORPORATION:

Secretary of State
Suite 1301 State Capitol
Lincoln, NE 68509
Tel.:402-471-4079
Fax: 402-471-3666
Website: www.nol.org/home/SOS/services.htm

What they supply:

State provides forms with instructions and a fee schedule on the Internet. For a successful download you need the Adobe® Acrobat Reader™.

What must be filed:

The completed form must be typewritten or printed. The document must be executed by an incorporator. The executing incorporator has to state her/his name and capacity ("incorporator") beneath or opposite the signature. Send the original and one copy to the secretary of state for filing. Make sure that you enclose the correct filing fee.

Name requirements:

The corporate name may not contain a word or a phrase which indicates that the corporation is organized for other than or more of the purposes contained in your articles of incorporation. The name may not be the same or deceptively similar to other registered corporations or reserved names.

Directors requirements:

Your corporation must have at least two directors. They don't have to be residents of Nebraska.

Articles requirements:

The articles have to include the following basic contents:
- the corporate name
- a statement about the general purpose of the corporation (public benefit corporation, mutual-benefit corporation or religious corporation)
- street address (post office box is not acceptable) of corporation's registered office and the name of its initial registered agent at that office
- name and street address of each incorporator
- a statement whether or not the corporation will have members
- provisions not consistent with the law regarding the distribution of assets on dissolution

Filing fees:

$10 plus $5 per page recording fee, payable to the Secretary of State.

Reports:

You have to file an annual report to January 1.

Statute: Chapter 21-1905 et seq., Nebraska Revised Statutes

TAXES:

Department of Revenue
P.O. Box 94818
Lincoln, NE 68509-4818
Tel.: 402-471-2971
Fax: 402-471-5608
Website: http://www.nol.org/home/NDR/

Automatic Exemption: Yes

CHARITABLE SOLICITATION:

Secretary of State
2300 State Capitol
Lincoln, NE 68509
Tel.: 402-471-2554

Statute:

Statutes 28-1440-1446 (unenforceable by a 1996 court decision—check the current status with the secretary of State), 28-1447-1449

Exemption: None

Annual Filing: No

Accept URS: Yes

NEVADA

INCORPORATION:

Secretary of State
Capitol Complex
Carson City, NV 89710
Tel.: 702-687-5203
Fax: 702-687-5071
or
Tel.: 702-687-5105
Website: www.sos.state.nv.us

What they supply:

State provides complete "Non-Profit Corporations Filing Packet" which contains fill-in-the-blanks forms of Articles of Incorporation and of a Certificate of Acceptance for the registered agents, filing instructions, a fee schedule and a list of registered agents.

What must be filed:

Type or print your Articles in black ink only. File the original and as many copies as you want to be certified and returned to you. Note that you must at least keep one certified copy in the office of your resident agent. Make sure that each incorporator's signature is notarized.

Name requirements:

Your corporate name may not appear to be that of a natural person and may not contain a given name or initials unless it is accompanied by one of the words "Corporation," "Corp.," "Incorporated," "Inc.," "Limited," "Ltd.," "Company," or "Co." The name may not be the same or deceptively similar to the name of any other corporation presently on file in Nevada.

For name availability check with the Secretary of State prior to filing by calling 702-687-5203.

Directors requirements:

Choose in Article 4 whether your Governing Board shall be styled as directors or trustees. Your Governing Board must at least have three members (directors or trustees).

Articles requirements:

Enter the name and address of your initial resident agent in Article 2 and make sure that agent signs the certificate of acceptance on the bottom of the page.

To characterize the purpose for which your corporation is formed in accordance to the IRS requirements check with the IRS prior to filing.

Give the names and addresses of your initial Governing Board in Article 4. Don't forget that each incorporator's signature is notarized.

Filing fees:

$25. Nevada offers an expedited filing service, which allows 24 hours filing. The additional fee for that service is $50.

Reports:

The fee for your corporation's annual report (annual list of officers & directors) is $15.

Statute: Chapter 82, Nevada Revised Statutes

TAXES:

Department of Taxation
Capitol Complex
Carson City, NV 89710-0003
Tel: 702-687-4892
Fax: 702-687-5981
Website: http://www.state.nv.us/taxation/

Automatic Exemption:

Yes (No state corporate income tax)

CHARITABLE SOLICITATION:

Secretary of State
Capitol Complex
Carson City, NV 89710
Tel.: 702-687-5203

Statute:

Nevada Revised Statutes, Chapter 598; Statutes of Nevada 1997, Chapter 692

Exemption:

No current registration requirements for solicitation of charitable contributions.

Annual filing: No

Accept URS: No

New Hampshire

INCORPORATION:

Secretary of State
State House, Room 204
107 N. Main St.
Concord, NH 03301
Tel.: 603-271-3244
Website: [none]

What they supply:

State provides fill-in-the-blanks forms of "Articles of Agreement" in duplicate plus filing instructions and statutory excerpts containing the most important statutes for filing your Articles.

What must be filed:

Print or type your documents in black ink and leave 1" margins on both sides.

File the original and one exact copy. Both documents must bear original signatures. Note that your Articles of Agreement must be filed with the clerk of the city/town of the principal place of business *prior* to filing with the Secretary of State. Enclose the filing fee.

Name requirements:

Your corporate name may not be the same or deceptively similar to an existing corporation name. For name availability call 603-271-3246 prior to filing.

Directors requirements:

Note that you need five or more incorporators to form a nonprofit corporation in New Hampshire but only one or more directors.

Articles requirements:

The most important requirement for forming your nonprofit corporation is that you need five or more incorporators.

The legal purposes your corporation may be formed for are listed in Chapter 292:1 of the Statutes provided by the State.

In Article 7 you have the opportunity to make provisions eliminating or limiting the personal liability of a director or officer of your corporation.

Filing fees:

The filing fee for the filing with the city/town clerk is $5, the fee for filing with the Secretary of State is $25.

Reports:

Your corporation must file the first report, called "return," in the year 2000 (regardless of the date of incorporation) and every five years thereafter. The fee for the return is $25.

Statutes:

Chapter 292 of the New Hampshire Revised Statutes

TAXES:

Department of Revenue Administration
61 S. Spring St.
P.O. Box 457
Concord, NH 03302-0637
Tel.: 603-271-2186
Fax: 603-271-2355
Website:
http://www.state.nh.us/revenue/revenue.htm

Automatic Exemption: Yes

CHARITABLE SOLICITATION:

Attorney General
Charitable Trust Division
33 Capitol Street
Concord, NH 03301-6397
Tel.: 603-271-3591

Statute: Revised Statutes Annotated 7:19

Exemption: None

Annual Filing: Yes

Accept URS: Yes

New Jersey

INCORPORATION:

Secretary of State
Division of Commercial Recording
Trenton, NJ 08625
Tel.: 609-530-6400
Website: www.state.nj.us/state/

What they supply:

State provides fill-in-the-blanks Certificate of Incorporation with filing instructions and a sample Certificate.

What must be filed:

Type your documents in black ink. File the original and two exact copies. Enclose a self-addressed stamped envelope to receive a filed copy and the correct filing fee.

Name requirements:

Your corporate name must include the words "A New Jersey Nonprofit Corporation," "Corporation," "Incorporated," "Inc.," or "Corp."

For name availability call 609-530-8312 prior to filing, a payment for name reservation can be made by credit card.

Directors requirements:

Your first board of directors (trustees) must have at least three members. They don't have to be residents of New Jersey.

Articles requirements:

To obtain the tax exempt status after filing your Articles make sure the purpose for which your corporation is organized (Article 2) will meet the IRS requirements for tax exemption.

You can leave most of the regulation for the corporations inner affairs to your by-laws if you don't want these affairs to be regulated by the Certificate of Incorporation.

Filing fees:

$50, payable to the Department of State. New Jersey offers an expedited service (filing complete within 8.5 hours) for an additional fee of $10. The expedited service request must be delivered either in person or by messenger service (FedEx or UPS—not U.S. Postal Overnight)

Reports:

The annual report form will be mailed to the registered agents office prior to the anniversary date of your corporation.

Statute: Title 15A:2-8, New Jersey Statutes

TAXES:

Department of Treasury
Division of Taxation
50 Barrack Street
CN-269
Trenton, NJ 08646
Tel.: 609-292-5994
Website: http://www.state.nj.us/treasury/revenue

Automatic Exemption: No

CHARITABLE SOLICITATION:

Charities Registration Section
P.O. Box 45021
Newark, NJ 07101
Tel.: 201-504-6259

Statute: New Jersey Statutes 45:17A, et seq.

Exemption: None

Annual filing: Yes

Accept URS: Yes

NEW MEXICO

INCORPORATION:

State Corporation Commission
Corporation Department
P.O. Drawer 1269
Santa Fe, NM 87504-1269
Tel.: 505-827-4511
    or
Tel.: 505-827-4504
Website: www.sos.state.nm.us/

What they supply:

State provides three copies of fill-in-the-blanks forms of Articles of Incorporation and of an affidavit of acceptance of appointment that has to be signed by the initial registered agent. Also filing instructions are provided.

What must be filed:

Type or print your Articles legibly in black ink. File duplicate originals and attach the completed, signed and notarized affidavit of acceptance of your registered agent. Enclose the correct filing fee.

Name requirements:

Your corporate name must not be the same or deceptively similar to any other company name already existing in New Mexico.

You can check for name availability by calling the Secretary of State at 505-827-4511.

Directors requirements:

Your corporation must have at least three directors. The directors do not have to be residents of New Mexico.

Articles requirements:

The minimum requirements for forming your corporation are as follows:
- the name of your corporation
- the period of its duration, which may be perpetual
- a definition of the purpose for which your corporation is formed
- provisions regulating the internal affairs of the corporation including provisions for distributing remaining assets upon the dissolution of the corporation
- the name of its initial agent and the address of the agent's office
- the number of persons serving as the initial directors and the names and addresses of these directors
- the name and address of each incorporator

Filing fees:

$25, payable to the "State Corporation Division." Only checks or cashier's checks are accepted. Certified copies are $10 each, if requested.

Reports:

You have to file an annual financial report due the 15th day of the 3rd month after the end of the fiscal year of the corporation.

Statute:

New Mexico Statutes Annotated, Chapter 53-8-31

TAXES:

Taxation and Revenue Department
P.O. Box 630
Santa Fe, NM 85709-0630
Tel.: 505-827-0700
Fax: 505-827-0469
Website: http://www.state.nm.us/tax/

Automatic Exemption: Yes

CHARITABLE SOLICITATION:

Office of the Attorney General
Charitable Organization Registry
P.O. Drawer 1508
Santa Fe, NM 87504-1508
Tel.: 505-827-6000

Statute:

New Mexico Statutes Annotated, 22:57-22-1, et seq.

Exemption: less than $2,500

Annual filing: Yes

Accept URS: Yes

NEW YORK

INCORPORATION:

Department of State
Division of Corporations and State Records
162 Washington Avenue
Albany, N.Y. 12231-0001
Tel.: 518-473-2492 or
Tel.: 518-474-6200
Website: www.dos.state.ny.us/

What they supply:

The office of the Secretary of State doesn't provide forms but an extract from the Not-For-Profit Corporation law with which you can draft your own Certificate of Incorporation. Forms can be obtained from legal stationery stores in New York State but it's not mandatory to use those forms.

What must be filed:

If you draft your own Articles of Incorporation (not using the forms) make sure that your documents contain a separate page which sets forth the title of the document being submitted and the name and address of the person to which the receipt for filing shall be mailed. Enclose the filing fee.

Name requirements:

Unless corporation is formed for religious purposes, the corporate name must contain the words "corporation," "incorporated," "limited," or an abbreviation of these words. A name reservation can be made for a fee of $10.

Directors requirements:

Your corporation must have at least three directors. They don't have to be residents of New York.

Articles requirements:

Your Certificate of Incorporation must set forth the following minimum:
- the name of the corporation
- a statement, that the corporation is formed pursuant to Subparagraph (a)(5) of section 102 of the Not-For-Profit Corporation Law, the type of corporation it shall be under section 201 (Type A - D) and the purpose for which the corporation is formed
- the county where the corporate office is to be located
- the name and address of each director, if your corporation is an A, B or C type corporation
- the duration of the corporation, if not perpetual
- a designation of the secretary of state as agent of the corporation upon whom process may be served and the p.o. address to which the secretary of state shall mail a copy on any process against it served upon him
- if applicable, the name of the registered agent and the address of its initial registered office and a statement, that he is the agent upon whom process against the corporation may be served
- any provision for the regulation of the internal affairs of the corporation that is not inconsistent with the law (e.g. types or classes of membership, distribution of assets upon dissolution)

Filing fees:

$75, payable to the Secretary of State. New York offers an expedited service (filing within 24 hours of receipt) for an additional $25—make sure to print "Attention: Expedited Handling" on the envelope.

Reports:

You have to file a report by request of the Secretary of State.

Statute:

NY Not-For-Profit Corporation Law, Sec. 402

TAXES:

State Department of Taxation and Finance
Technical Service Bureau
Building 9, Room 104, State Campus
Albany, NY 12227
Tel.: 518-457-6139
Fax: 518-457-2486
Website: http://www.tax.state.ny.us/

Automatic Exemption: No

CHARITABLE SOLICITATION:

Office of the Attorney General
Charities Bureau
120 Broadway
New York, NY 10271
Tel.: 212-416-8400

Statute: Art 7-A, Executive Law

Exemption: 25,000 and unpaid fundraising

Annual filing: Yes

Accept URS: Yes

NORTH CAROLINA

INCORPORATION:

Corporations Division
Department of Secretary of State
300 North Salisbury Street
Raleigh, NC 27603-5909
Tel.: 919-733-4201
Website: www.state.nc.us/secstate/

What they supply:

State doesn't provide fill-in-the-blanks forms but a booklet "North Carolina Non-Profit Corporation Guidelines" which contains samples of Articles of Incorporation, Articles of Amendment and other documents needed for maintaining a corporation.

The booklet also includes general information about incorporating in North Carolina. It also gives instructions how to apply for the federal tax exemption.

What must be filed:

Draft your articles accordingly to the sample and the instructions given in the booklet. File the original and one exact copy together with the filing fee.

After filing the copy will be returned "file-stamped" to the incorporator(s).

Name requirements:

The booklet contains a comprehensive chapter about how to select and determine a corporate name. Your corporate name must be distinguishable from any other corporate name already on record with the Secretary of State. You can call or write to the Secretary of State prior to filing whether the name you want to use is available. A name reservation can be made for a fee of $10.

Directors requirements:

Your corporation is required to have at least one director. He has not to be a resident of North Carolina.

Articles requirements:

Your Articles of Incorporation require the following minimum:

- the corporate name
- a statement, whether your corporation shall be a "charitable or religious corporation" pursuant to the N.C. General Statutes 55A-2-02 (a)(2)

- the name of your initial registered agent and the street address of its initial registered office (if mailing address is different, give the mailing address)
- the name and address of each incorporator (at least one incorporator required)
- a statement whether your corporation shall have members
- provisions regarding the distribution of assets upon the dissolution of the corporation
- the street address (and, if different, the mailing address) and county of your principal office
- the signature and capacity of each incorporator

Filing fees:

$60, payable to the Secretary of State. There's an expedited service available for:

- an additional $ 200 for filing on the same day (documents must be received by 12:00 noon)
- an additional $ 100 for filing within 24 hours

Reports:

An annual report is not required.

Statute:

North Carolina General Statutes, Chapter 55A

TAXES:

Department of Revenue
P.O. Box 25000
Raleigh, NC 27640
Tel.: 919-733-3166
Website: http://www.dor.state.nc.us/DOR/

Automatic Exemption: No

CHARITABLE SOLICITATION:

Solicitation Licensing Branch
701 Balbour Drive
P.O. Box 29530
Raleigh, NC 27603
Tel.: 919-733-4510

Statute:

North Carolina General Statutes, Chapter 131F

Exemption:

less than $25,000 if nobody is paid to fundraise

Annual filing: Yes

Accept URS: No

NORTH DAKOTA

INCORPORATION:

Secretary of State
Capitol Building
600 East Boulevard Avenue
Bismarck, ND 58505-0500
Tel.: 701-328-4284
Fax: 701-328-2992
Website: www.state.nd.us/sec

What they supply:

State provides fill-in-the-blanks form of Articles of Incorporation and a Consent to Serve form to be signed by the registered agent.

What must be filed:

Complete your Articles and file in duplicate. Attach the signed consent to serve and enclose the filing fee for the articles and for the consent.

Name requirements:

Your corporate name must be distinguishable from any other corporate name already on file with the Secretary of State.

Directors requirements:

Your corporation must at least have three directors. They don't have to be residents of North Dakota.

Articles requirements:

Your Articles require the following minimum:
- the name of your corporation
- if not perpetual, the duration of its existence
- a specific characterization of the purpose for which the corporation is formed
- provisions for the distribution of assets upon the dissolution or final liquidation of the corporation
- the name of the initial registered agent and the address of the agent's registered office
- the number of your initial directors and their names and addresses

Filing fees:

$30 for filing the articles, another $ 10 for filing the consent, both fees have to be paid.

Reports: An annual report is not required.

Statute:

Chapter 10-33, North Dakota Century Code

TAXES:

State Tax Department
600 E. Boulevard Ave.
Bismarck, ND 58505
Tel.: 701-224-2045
Fax: 800-472-2110
Website: http://www.state.nd.us/taxdpt

Automatic Exemption: Yes

CHARITABLE SOLICITATION:

Secretary of State
State Capitol Building
Bismarck, ND 58505
Tel.: 701-224-2905

Statute:

Chapter 50-22, North Dakota Century Code

Exemption: None

Annual Filing: Yes

Accept URS: Yes

OHIO

INCORPORATION:

Secretary of State
Corporations Division
30 E. Broad St.
State Office Tower, 14th Floor
Columbus, OH 43266-0418
Tel.: 614-466-3910
Website: www.state.oh.us/sos/

What they supply:

State provides fill-in-the-blanks articles, a separate form for the registered agent and a booklet with all important information about Nonprofit Organizations in Ohio.

What must be filed:

Complete the fill-in-the-blanks articles and file them with the Secretary of State. Make sure that the articles are signed by the incorporators and their names are printed or typed beneath their signatures. Enclose the filing fee. The trustees don't have to sign the articles.

Name requirements:

The name of the corporation is not required to have an corporate ending (e.g. Inc., Corp.). It may be not the same or deceptively similar to another corporation under the law of Ohio.

Directors requirements:

Your corporation must have not less than three directors. They don't have to be residents of Ohio.

Articles requirements:

The basic requirements are as follows:

- the corporate name
- the names and addresses of the initial trustees (not fewer than three natural persons)
- name and address of a statutory agent
- the specific purpose of the corporation (a general purpose clause will not be accepted)

Filing fee:

$25, payable to the Secretary of State

Reports:

You have to file an statement of continued existence each five years. You will get a written notice and the necessary forms from the Secretary of State.

Statute: Ohio Revised Code, Chapter 1702.04

TAXES:

Secretary of State
Corporate Income Tax Division
30 E. Broad Street, 14th Floor
Columbus, OH 43266-0418
Tel.: 614-846-6712
Website: http://www.state.oh.us/tax/

Automatic Exemption: Yes

CHARITABLE SOLICITATION:

Attorney General
Charitable Foundation Section
101 E. Town Street, 4th Floor
Columbus, OH 43266-0900
Tel.: 614-466-3180

Statute: Ohio Revised Code, Chapter 1716

Exemption:

$25,000, provided the corporation does not compensate any person primarily to solicit.

Annual filing: Yes

Accept URS: Yes

OKLAHOMA

INCORPORATION:

Secretary of State-Corporation Division
2300 N. Lincoln Blvd.
101 State Capitol Building
Oklahoma City, OK 73105
Tel.: 405-521-3911
Website: www.occ.state.ok.us/

What they supply:

State provides two fill-in-the-blanks copies of Certificate of Incorporation and instructions how to file.

What must be filed:

Type or print your documents clearly and file the original in duplicate. Enclose the filing fee.

Name requirements:

Your corporate name must contain one of the following words or abbreviations: "association, company, corporation, club, foundation, fund, incorporated, institute, society, union, syndicate, limited, co., corp., inc. or ltd."

For name availability check with the Corporate Filing Division at 405-522-4560 prior to filing. A corporate name can be reserved by filing a name reservation application with a fee of $10 for a period of sixty days.

Directors requirements:

Your corporation must at least have one director or trustee. He does not have to be resident of Oklahoma.

Articles requirements:

The basic requirements are as follows:
- the corporate name
- the name of your initial registered agent and the address of its initial registered office
- if your corporation is a church, the street address of its location

- if not perpetual, the duration of your corporation
- the specific purpose for which your corporation is formed
- the number, names and mailing addresses of your initial directors
- the names and mailing address of each incorporator

Make sure that each incorporator signs the articles.

Filing fees:

$25, payable to the Secretary of State.

Reports:

You have to file an annual report by March 31.

Statute:

Title 18, Section 1001 of the Oklahoma General Corporation Act

TAXES:

Oklahoma Tax Commission
2501 Lincoln Boulevard
Oklahoma City, OK 73194
Tel.: 405-521-1350
Website: http:/www.oktax.state.ok.us/oktax/

Automatic Exemption: Yes

CHARITABLE SOLICITATION:

Attorney General
4545 N. Lincoln Boulevard, Suite 250
Oklahoma City, OK 73105-3498
Tel.: 405-521-4274

Statute: O.S. Title 18:552, et seq.

Exemption: less than $10,000

Annual filing: Yes

Accept URS: Yes

OREGON

INCORPORATION:

Corporation Division
State of Oregon
158 -12th St. NE
Salem, OR 97310
Tel.: 503-986-2200
Fax: 503-378-4381
Website: www.sos.state.or.us/

What they supply:

State provides complete business package including the "Oregon Business Guide," which gives detailed information on all kinds of businesses. The package also includes tax tables, an Employer's Registration form, and an application for the Employer Identification Number (IRS form SS-4). To obtain more information about non-profit corporations, call the state's toll-free helpline at 888-206-3076.

What must be filed:

Type or print the articles in black ink. If you file your documents by mail, attach one exact copy of the original. Enclose the filing fee.

Name requirements:

Your corporate name must contain the words "corporation," incorporated," "company," "limited," or an abbreviation of these words. The name must be distinguishable from other active names on Business Records. For name availability call 503-986-2200. For a name reservation send an application and a $10 fee to the filing office. If the name is available, it will be reserved for 120 days.

Directors requirements:

A certain number of directors is not required, but you have to fix the number of initial directors in your articles and the number of subsequent directors in the bylaws.

Articles requirements:

The basic requirements are as follows:
- Corporate name
- name and address of registered agent (the address must be an Oregon street address and identical with the agent's business office, post office boxes are not acceptable)
- additional the agent's mailing address
- corporation's address for mailing notices
- type of corporation (Public Benefit, Mutual Benefit, Religious)
- a statement whether the corporation will have members or not
- a statement concerning the distribution of assets upon dissolution
- names and addresses of all incorporators

Make sure that each incorporator signs the document and print or typewrite the names beneath the signatures.

Filing fees:

$20 for filing the articles, payable to the "Corporation Division." Fees can be paid by check or by Visa or Mastercard.

Reports:

The annual report must be delivered to the secretary of state on the anniversary date of your corporation. The annual report form is sent to the registered agent 45 days prior to the due date. The annual fee is $10.

Statute:

Chapter 65 Oregon Revised Statutes, Oregon Business Corporation Act

TAXES:

Department of Revenue
955 Center St. NE
Salem, OR 97310
503-378-3725
Website: http://www.dor.state.or.us

Automatic Exemption: Yes

CHARITABLE SOLICITATION:

Attorney General
Administrator of Charitable Trusts
1515 S.W. 5th Avenue, Suite 410
Portland, OR 97201
Tel.: 503-229-5548

Statute: Oregon Revised Statutes 128.610 - 129

Exemption: None

Annual filing: Yes

Accept URS: Yes

PENNSYLVANIA

INCORPORATION:

Department of State
Corporation Bureau
P. O. Box 8722
Harrisburg, PA 17105-8722
Tel.: 717-787-1057
Website: www.dos.state.pa.us/corp.htm

What they supply:

The State provides fill-in-the-blanks Articles of Incorporation with filing instructions and a fill-in-the-blanks docketing statement that has to be filed with your articles.

What must be filed:

Print or type your documents in black or blue-black ink. File the original of your articles of incorporation, attach a cover letter and enclose the following:

- three copies of the completed docketing statement (form DSCB: 15-134A)—this form is provided by the state
- if applicable, copies of the Consent to Appropriation of Name or, copies of the Consent to Use of Similar Name
- the filing fee

Also include either a self-addressed, stamped postcard with the filing information noted or a self-addressed, stamped envelope with a copy of the filing document to receive confirmation of the file date prior to receiving the microfilmed original.

Name requirements:

Your corporate name must include the words "incorporated," "corporation," "company," "limited," "fund," "association," "syndicate," or an abbreviation of these words.

Name availability can be checked either by a written request or by phone at 717-787-1057. The fee for an availability of three names is $12.

A name reservation can only be made by a written request together with a $52 fee. The reservation is good for 120 days. Your will get a confirmation of your reservation by mail.

Directors requirements:

If you do not specify the number of directors in your By-laws, the minimum number is three, otherwise one.

Articles requirements:

If you want to apply for the federal tax exemption, check with the IRS prior to filing your articles to make sure your corporation meets the special purpose required to qualify for the tax exemption (purpose must be given in Article 3)

Give the name and address of each incorporator in Article 8 (minimum of one incorporator).

Filing fees: $100, payable to the Dept. of State.

Reports:

An annual report must only be filed if there's any change of the corporation's officers. If your corporation must file such a report, there's no filing fee.

Statute: 15 Pa. C.S

TAXES:

Department of Revenue
Bureau of Corporation Taxes
P.O. Box 8911
Harrisburg, PA 17127
Tel.: 717-783-6035
Website: http://www.revenue.state.pa.us/

Automatic Exemption: No

CHARITABLE SOLICITATION:

Department of State
Bureau of Charitable Organizations
P.O. Box 8723
Harrisburg, PA 17150
Tel.: 717-783-1720

Statute: 10 Pa. S. 162.1 et seq.

Exemption:

less than $25,000 annually provided nobody is paid to fundraise

Annual filing: Yes

Accept URS: Yes

RHODE ISLAND

INCORPORATION:

Secretary of State
100 N. Main St.
Providence, RI 02903
Tel.: 401-222-3040
Fax: 401-277-1309
Website: www.state.ri.us/corporations

What they supply:

State provides original and duplicate fill-in-the-blanks Articles of Incorporation with filing instructions.

What must be filed:

Complete and sign the original and the duplicate articles. Enclose the filing fee.

When the articles are properly completed, a Certificate of Incorporation, together with the file stamped original will be returned to you.

Name requirements:

The name may not be the same or deceptively similar to any other entity name already on file with the Corporations Division.

For name availability check prior to filing by calling the Corporations Division at the phone number given above.

Directors requirements:

Your corporation must have at least three directors. They don't have to be residents of Rhode Island.

Articles requirements:

The minimum requirements are as follows:

- the corporate name
- if not perpetual, the duration of the corporation
- the specific purpose your corporation is formed for (if you want to apply for the federal tax exemption, check with the IRS prior to filing if your corporation must meet specific requirements)
- any provisions for regulating the corporation's internal affairs

- the name of the initial registered agent and the address of its initial registered office
- the number of directors and their names and addresses
- the name and address of each incorporator

Make sure that each incorporator signs the articles.

Filing fees:

$35, payable to the Secretary of State.

Reports:

An annual report must be filed each calendar year in the month of June beginning the year following the year of incorporation.

Statute:

Chapter 7-6-34 of the General Laws of Rhode Island

TAXES:

Department of Administration
Division of Taxation
289 Promenade Street
Providence, RI 02908
Tel.: 401-277-2905
Fax: 401-277-6006
Website: http://www.tax.state.ri.us/

Automatic Exemption: Yes

CHARITABLE SOLICITATION:

Department of Business Regulations
Charitable Organization Section
233 Richmond Street, Suite 232
Providence, RI 02903-4232
Tel.: 401-277-3048

Statute: R.I.G.L. Title 5, Chapter 53

Exemption: $3000 or 10 or less donors in a year

Annual filing: Yes

Accept URS: Yes

SOUTH CAROLINA

INCORPORATION:

Secretary of State
P.O. Box 11350
Columbia, SC 29211
Tel.: 803-734-2158
Web site: www.leginfo.state.sc.us/secretary.html

What they supply:

State provides fill-in-the-blanks Articles of Incorporation with brief instructions.

What must be filed:

File the completed original and either a duplicate original or a conformed copy. Enclose the filing fee.

Name requirements:

Your corporate name must include the words "corporation," "incorporated," "company," "limited," or an abbreviation of these words. It must be distinguishable from any other business name already on file with the Secretary of State.

A name can be reserved for 120 days for a fee of $25.

Directors requirements:

Your corporation must have at least one director. He or she doesn't have to be a resident of South Carolina.

Articles requirements:

In Article 3 check the appropriate box whether your corporation is a public benefit, religious or mutual benefit corporation. If you want to apply for the federal tax exemption and your corporation is either a public benefit or religious corporation, check the "a" box in Article 6 to make sure that upon dissolution of the corporation, the assets will be distributed accordingly to the tax exempt purposes. If you form a mutual benefit corporation check one of the two dissolution statements in Article 7.

Each incorporator (minimum of one) must sign the articles.

Filing fees:

$25, payable to the Secretary of State.

Reports:

You have to file an annual report by the 15th day of the 3rd month after the end of the corporation's fiscal year

Statute:

Chapter 33-44 of the South Carolina Code of 1976

TAXES:

South Carolina Tax Commission
P.O. Box 125
Columbia, SC 29214
Tel.: 803-737-5000
Fax: 803-737-9881
Website: http://www.dor.state.sc.us/

Automatic Exemption: Yes

CHARITABLE SOLICITATION:

Secretary of State
Director of Public Charities
P.O. Box 11350
Columbia, SC 29211
Tel.: 803-734-2168

Statute: South Carolina Code 33-56-10

Exemption: $5,000

Annual filing: Yes

Accept URS: Yes

SOUTH DAKOTA

INCORPORATION:

Secretary of State
State Capital
500 E. Capital Street
Pierre, SD 57501
Tel.: 605-773-4845
Fax: 605-773-4550
Website:
www.state.sd.us/state/executive/sos/sos.htm

What they supply:

State provides fill-in-the-blanks-form of Articles of Incorporation, a small booklet "Domestic Nonprofit Corporations" and a copy of the Nonprofit Statutes.

What must be filed:

Type your articles and file the original document and one exact copy. Make sure that the consent of Appointment is signed by your registered agent. and that your articles are notarized. Enclose the filing fee.

Name requirements:

Your corporate name may not be the same or deceptively similar to the name of any other corporation registered in the State of South Dakota.

For name availability check with the Secretary of State at the phone number given above. A name can be reserved for a period of 120 days for a fee of $15.

Directors requirements:

Your Board of Directors must have at least three members. The directors do not have to be residents of South Dakota.

Articles requirements:

Your articles must contain the following minimum:
- the name of the corporation
- if not perpetual, the period of existence
- the purpose for which the corporation is formed— this clause must contain sufficient information to determine the type of purpose. Types of purposes are given in Section 47-22-4 of the Statutes.
- a statement whether the corporation shall have members and if so, provisions regulating the class of members and their rights
- regulations concerning the method of election of the directors
- any provisions regulating the internal affairs of the corporation
- the street address of your initial registered office and the name or your initial registered agent
- the number of directors and their names and addresses
- the names and addresses of the incorporators (minimum of three)
- the signature of each incorporator

Filing fees:

$20, payable to the Secretary of State.

Reports:

A report containing the basic information about your corporation has to be filed every three years by the first day of the second month following the anniversary month of the corporation. The Secretary of State will provide forms for filing this report prior to the due date. The filing fee for the report is $10.

Statute:

Chapter 47 of the South Dakota Codified Laws

TAXES:

Department of Revenue
700 Governors Dr.
Pierre, SD 57501-2276
Tel.: 605-773-5141
Fax: 605-773-5129
Website: http://www.state.sd.us/state/executive/revenue/revenue.html

Automatic Exemption: Yes

CHARITABLE SOLICITATION:

Attorney General
State Capitol
500 East Capitol
Pierre, SD 57501-5070
Tel.: 605-773-4400

Statute:

South Dakota Codified Laws, Title 37, Chapter 30 (regulates only solicitation of charitable contributions by telephone)

Exemption: None

Annual filing: No

Accept URS: No

TENNESSEE

INCORPORATION:

Department of State
Division of Services
Suite 1800
James K. Polk Building
Nashville, TN 37243-0306
Tel.: 615-741-0537
Fax: 615-741-7310
Website: www.state.tn.us/sos/
email address: rgrunow@mail.state.tn.us

What they supply:

Provides a comprehensive and detailed "Filing Guide" for Nonprofit Corporations, a filing fee schedule, and a fill-in-the-blanks Charter (Articles of Incorporation).

What must be filed:

Type or print your articles in black ink using either the fill-in-the-blanks form or, if drafting your own documents, using legal or letter size paper. The documents must be executed either by an incorporator, by the chair of the board of directors or by a trustee. File only the original document(s) together with the filing fee.

Name requirements:

Your corporate name must be distinguishable from any other name on file with the Division of Business Services, the filing guide provides sufficient information, whether or not names are distinguishable from others. It may not contain language implying that the corporation transacts business for which authorization is required or that the corporation is organized as a fraternal, veterans, service, religious, charitable or professional organization.

For name availability call 615-741-0537 prior to filing, a name reservation can be made by filing an application with the Division of Business Services together with a $20 fee.

Directors requirements:

Your corporation must have at least 3 directors. They don't have to be residents of Tennessee.

Articles requirements:

Your charter must contain the following minimum:
• the corporate name

• a statement whether the corporation is a public or mutual benefit corporation or whether it's a religious corporation
• the address of the initial registered office and the name of the initial registered agent
• the name and address of each incorporator
• the street address of the principal office (may be the same as the address of the registered agent)
• a statement that the corporation is not for profit
• a statement that there will be no members
• provisions regarding the distribution of assets upon the dissolution of the corporation

Filing fees:

$100, payable to the Division of Business Services.

Reports:

The annual report must be filed on or before the first day of the fourth month following the close of the corporation's fiscal year. The report form will be sent to the registered office one month prior to the end of the corporation's fiscal year. The fee for the annual report is $ 20.

Statute:

Tennessee Nonprofit Corporation Act, Section 48-52

TAXES:

Tennessee Department of Revenue
Andrew Jackson Office Bldg.
500 Deaderick Street
Nashville, TN 37242-1099
Tel.: 615-741-3133
Fax: 615-741-0682
Website: http://www.state.tn.us/revenue/

Automatic Exemption: Yes

CHARITABLE SOLICITATION:

Secretary of State
James K. Polk Bldg., Suite 500
Nashville, TN 37243-0308
Tel.: 615-741-2555

Statute: TCA 48-101-501 et seq.

Exemption: $30,000

Annual filing: Yes

Accept URS: Yes

TEXAS

INCORPORATION:

Secretary of State
Corporation Division
P.O. Box 13697
Austin, TX 78711
Tel.: 512-463-5555
Tel.: 900-263-0060 (to obtain forms)
Website: www.sos.state.tx.us/

What they supply:

State provides guidelines to draft your own Articles of Incorporation (a so-called "Nonprofit Corporation Summary," form 202).

What must be filed:

Draft your own Articles accordingly to the instructions provided by the state. File two copies of these together with the filing fee. The filing office will return one filed stamped copy.

Name requirements:

Your corporate name may include words like "corporation," "incorporated," or "company," but it's not mandatory.

For name availability call prior to filing 512-463-5555, a name reservation can be made for a fee of $25 for a period of 120 days.

Directors requirements:

Your corporation may not have less than three directors. They don't have to be residents of Texas.

Articles requirements:

The minimum contents of your articles are as follows:

- the name of your corporation
- the period of duration, which may be perpetual
- a statement that your corporation is not for profit
- the specific purpose for which your corporation is formed (check with the IRS prior to filing what requirements your corporation has to meet to qualify for the federal tax exemption)
- the name of the registered agent and the address of your registered office.

- a statement whether corporation shall have members
- if the management of your corporation shall be vested in the members, a statement to that effect
- the number of your initial board of directors and the names and addresses of your directors
- the name and street address of each incorporator
- provisions regarding the distribution of assets upon the dissolution of the corporation

Make sure that each incorporator signs the articles.

Filing fees: $25, payable to the Secretary of State.

Reports:

You have to file a report upon request from the Secretary of State (once every four years). The Secretary of State will send notice and the necessary forms before the report is due.

Statute: Article 1396-3.02 of the Texas Non-Profit Corporation Act

TAXES:

Office of the Comptroller
Exempt Organizations
111 W. 6th Street
Austin, TX 78701
Tel.: 512-463-4142
Website: http://www.window.state.tx.us

Automatic Exemption: No

CHARITABLE SOLICITATION:

Attorney General
Charitable Trust Section
P.O. Box12548
Austin, TX 78711
Tel.: 512-463-2185

Statute:

Texas does not have a general statute, but certain cities have special requirements for solicitation of charitable contributions.

Exemption:

No current state registration requirements for solicitation of charitable contribution

Annual filing: No

Accept URS: No

UTAH

INCORPORATION:

Department of Commerce
Division of Corporations and Commercial Code
P.O. Box 45801
160 E. 300 South, 2nd Floor
Salt Lake City, UT 84145-0801
Tel.: 801-530-4849
Website: www.ce.ex.state.ut.us/nav/library

What they supply:

State provides guidelines how to draft your own articles of organization, a certain form is not necessary. They also send you a booklet "Doing business in Utah" which contains information about how to start or expand a business, the different business forms and tax aspects. The booklet also includes a directory of agencies and offices.

What must be filed:

File one original and one exact copy of your self-drafted articles. At least one document must bear the original signature. You can deliver the documents personally, by mail or even by fax. If you choose to fax your documents, make sure to include the number of your Visa / Mastercard and the expiration date.

Name requirements:

There are no special name requirements for your corporate name, although the name may contain the words "corporation" or "incorporated." The corporate name must be distinguishable from any other corporate name already on file with the Secretary of State.

Directors requirements:

Your corporation must at least have three trustees. They don't have to be residents of Utah or member of the corporation.

Articles requirements:

The minimum of what your articles must contain is:
- the corporate name
- the term of the corporation's existence
- the purpose or purposes for which your corporation is formed—this must include the statement that it is organized as a non-profit corporation
- the address of the corporation's principal office

- a statement whether or not the corporation shall have members
- the number of initial trustees your corporation shall have and their names and addresses
- the name and street address of each incorporator (at least one)
- the name of the corporation's initial registered agent and the street address of the registered office
- the signature of each incorporator

Your articles also must include a statement by your registered agent that he/she acknowledges his/her acceptance as registered agent.

Filing fees: $20, payable to the Secretary of State.

Reports:

The annual report must be filed in the month of the anniversary date the corporation was created. The Division of Corporations sends an annual report notice and a reporting form to the registered agent prior to the filing date.

Statute:

Utah Code Annotated, Corporation Laws Section 16-6-46

TAXES:

Utah State Tax Commission
160 E. 300 S
P.O. Box 4000
Salt Lake City, UT 84134
Tel.:801-530-4848
Website: http://www.txdtm01.tax.ex.state.ut.us/

Automatic Exemption: No

CHARITABLE SOLICITATION:

Department of Commerce
Division of Consumer Protection
P.O. Box 45802
Salt Lake City, UT 84145-0802
Tel.: 801-530-6601

Statute:

Utah Code, Title 13, Chapter 22, Section 1-22

Exemption: None

Annual Filing: Yes

Accept URS: No

VERMONT

INCORPORATION:

Secretary of State
109 State St.
Montpelier, VT 05609-1104
Tel.: 802-828-2363
Website: www.sec.state.vt.us/

What they supply:

State provides fill-in-the-blanks form of Articles of Incorporation for non-profit corporations with (little) instructions.

What must be filed:

Complete the fill-in-the-blanks form by typewriting or printing. File the original and one exact copy. Enclose the filing fee.

Name requirements:

Your corporate name must end with the words "corporation," "incorporated," "company," "limited," or "cooperative"(if applicable).
A name can be reserved for 120 days for a fee of $20.

Directors requirements:

Your corporation must have at least three directors, if you form a marketing cooperative, it must have at least five directors.

Articles requirements:

The minimum requirements are as follows:
- the corporate name
- the name of the registered agent
- the street address of your registered office
- if not perpetual, the period of duration
- a statement, whether your corporation shall be a public benefit, mutual benefit non-profit corporation or a cooperative.
- the names and addresses of your initial directors

- if applicable, the names and addresses of your members
- the specific purpose for which your corporation is formed
- provisions regarding the distribution of assets upon the dissolution of the corporation
- signatures and addresses of each incorporator

Filing fees:

$75, payable to the "Vermont Secretary of State."

Reports:

Non-profit corporations must file biennial reports. The Secretary of State will send notice before the report is due.

Statute: Title 11, VSA, Nonprofit Corporations

TAXES:

Department of Taxes
Agency of Administration
Pavilion Office Building
Montpelier, VT 05602
Tel.: 802-828-2551
Website: http://www.state.vt.us/tax

Automatic Exemption: No

CHARITABLE SOLICITATION:

Attorney General
Pavilion Office Building
Montpelier, VT 05602
Tel.: 802-828-3171

Statute:

Vermont Statutes, Chapter 63, Title 9, Section 2471, et seq.

Exemption:

Only the paid solicitor needs to register. Otherwise, there are no current requirements for solicitation.

Annual filing: No

Accept URS: No

VIRGINIA

INCORPORATION:

State Corporation Commission
Jefferson Building
P.O. Box 1197
Richmond, VA 23219
Tel.: 804-371-9733
Website: www.state.va.us/scc/index.html

What they supply:

State provides a filing booklet "Business Registration Guide" which contains filing instructions and tear out forms for all different kinds of business entities and tax forms. Note that the instructions are on the reverse side of the tear out forms.

What must be filed:

For forming a non-profit corporation take form SCC 819 (non stock corporation). Typewrite your articles in black ink. Complete and file only the original form and enclose the filing fee.

Name requirements:

There are no special requirements for your corporate name but it must not be the same or deceptively similar to any other corporate name existing in Virginia.

Directors requirements:

If you want your corporation to have initial directors, the minimum number is one. Each initial director has to be named in the articles.

Articles requirements:

The minimum requirements for filing your articles are as follows:
- the corporate name
- a statement whether or not your corporation shall have members and if so, provisions designating the classes of members and their rights
- a statement of the manner in which directors shall be elected or appointed
- the name of your initial registered agent and its status
- the address of your registered office
- optional provisions regarding the purpose for which your corporation is formed. To meet the special requirements for obtaining the federal tax exempt status, check with the IRS prior to filing your articles which requirements have to be met
- if your corporation shall have initial directors, state the number of directors and their names and addresses
- the signature and printed name of each incorporator

Filing fees:

$75 (including $50 charter fee and $25 filing fee), payable to the State Corporation Commission (pay by check or similar payment method, no cash accepted)

Reports:

The annual report must be filed between January 1 and April 1 with a small registration fee. The Secretary of State will send a report form prior to the due date.

Statute: Code of Virginia, Chapter 10 of Title 13.1

TAXES:

Department of Taxation
P.O. Box 6-L
Richmond, VA 23282
Fax: 804-367-2062
Website: http://www.tax.state.va.us/

Automatic Exemption: Yes

CHARITABLE SOLICITATION:

Division of Consumer Affairs
P.O. Box 1163
Richmond, VA 23209
Tel.: 804-786-1343

Statute: Code of Virginia, 57-48 to 57-69

Exemption:

$5,000 provided all corporation's activities are carried out by volunteers

Annual filing: Yes

Accept URS: Yes

WASHINGTON

INCORPORATION:

Secretary of State
Corporation Division
P.O. Box 40234
Olympia, WA 98504-0234
Tel.: 360-753-7115
Website: www.secstate.wa.gov

What they supply:

State provides a single fill-in-the-blanks form of Articles of Incorporation without any instructions. Also, a filing fee schedule is provided.

What must be filed:

Type or print the document in black ink. Submit the original and one copy together with the filing fee.

An expedited service (filing within 24 hours) is available for an extra $20 fee. If you want the expedited service write "expedited" in bold letters on outside of envelope.

Name requirements:

Your corporate name may not contain words like "corporation," "incorporated," "limited," or abbreviations "corp.," "inc.," or "ltd.;" but it may contain designations such as "Association," "Services," or "Committee."

For a fee of $20 you can reserve a corporate name for a period of 180 days.

Directors requirements:

Your corporation must have one or more directors. He doesn't have to be resident of Washington.

Articles requirements:

At a minimum, your articles must contain the following:

- the name of the corporation
- if wanted, a specific effective date of incorporation
- the term of existence
- the purpose for which the corporation is formed
- provisions regulating the distribution of assets upon dissolution of the corporation
- the name and street address of the initial registered agent and a signature by this agent, acknowledging his acceptance
- the name and address of each initial director
- the name and address of each incorporator
- the signature of each incorporator

Filing fees: $30, payable to the Secretary of State.

Reports:

Your annual report has to be filed between January 1 and March 1 each year. The fee is $10. The report form is provided by the Secretary of State.

Statute: Chapter 24.03 RCW

TAXES:

State Department of Revenue
General Administration Building
AX-02
Olympia, WA 98504-0090
Tel.: 206-753-5540
Website: http://dor.wa.gov/index.asp?

Automatic Exemption: Yes

CHARITABLE SOLICITATION:

Office of the Secretary of State
Corporations Division
P.O. Box 40234
Olympia, WA 98504-02234
Tel.: 360-753-0863

Statute: RCW Chapter 19.09 et seq.

Exemption:

less than $25,000, provided all corporation's activities are carried out by unpaid persons.

Annual filing: Yes

Accept URS: Yes

WEST VIRGINIA

INCORPORATION:

Secretary of State
State Capital
Charleston, WV 25305
Tel.: 304-558-8000
Fax: 304-558-0900
Website: www.state.wv.us/sos (a special website of the corporate division is under construction)

What they supply:

State provides duplicate copy of fill-in-the-blanks Articles of Incorporation and filing instructions.

What must be filed:

Complete the articles and file both originals. Make sure that the incorporator(s) file both documents and that the documents are notarized. Enclose the filing fee.

Name requirements:

Your corporate name must include the words "corporation," "company," "limited," "incorporated," or an abbreviation of these words. The name may not contain any word or phrase which implies that it is organized for any purposes other than those contained in the articles of incorporation.

Name availability can be checked by calling the Secretary of State at the phone number given above. A name reservation can be made by a written application accompanied by a $15 fee. The reservation is good for 120 days.

Directors requirements:

Your corporation must have at least one director. The director does not have to be a resident of West Virginia or a member of the corporation.

Articles requirements:

The fill-in-the-blanks form provided by the State is both for stock and non-stock (non-profit) corporations. Check the "non-profit" box in Article 5 to denote your corporation structure. Then state the purpose your corporation is formed for in Article 7 and check the appropriate box whether provisions regulating the internal affairs of the corporation shall be set forth in the bylaws or are attached to the articles. Give the names and street addresses of the incorporators in Article 10 and the names and number of initial directors in Article 11. Name at least one person who shall have signature authority on documents filed with the Secretary of State (annual report). The incorporators must sign the articles. Make sure that the signatures are notarized.

Filing fees:

The registration fee for non-profit corporations is $25. An additional "Attorney-in-fact fee," which depends on the month your articles will be received by the Secretary of State, is also required. Check the fee schedule to find out about the correct additional fee.

Reports:

Your first annual report must be filed between January 1 and March 31 of the first calendar year succeeding the date of incorporation. Thereafter, the reports are due between January 1 and March 31 each year.

Statute: West Virginia Code Section 31-1-27

TAXES:

West Virginia Tax Department
Taxpayer Service Division
P.O. Drawer 3784
Charleston, WV 25337-3784
Tel.: 800-642-9016 (in West Virginia)
Fax.: 304-558-2501
Website: http://www.state.wv.us/taxrev/

Automatic Exemption: Yes

CHARITABLE SOLICITATION:

Attorney General
Consumer Protection Division
P.O. Box 1789
Charleston, WV 25326-1789
Tel.: 304-558-8986

Statue: West Virginia Code, Chapter 29, Art. 19

Exemption:

Following organizations provided they don't employ a professional fundraiser and don't receive contributions in excess of $10,000 during a calender year:
- local youth athletic organizations
- community civic or service clubs
- fraternal organizations and labor unions
- local posts, camps, chapters or similarly designated elements or county units of such elements of bona fide veteran's organizations or auxiliaries which issue charters to such local elements throughout the state
- bona fide organizations of volunteer firemen, ambulance, rescue squads or auxiliaries

Annual filing: Yes

Accept URS: No

WISCONSIN

INCORPORATION:

Department of Financial Institutions
Division of Corporate & Consumer Services
345 W. Washington Ave., 3rd floor
Madison, WI 53703
Tel.: 608-261-7577
Website: www.state.wi.us/agencies/sos
or for download: www.wdfi.org/corp/forms.htm

What they supply:

State provides fill-in-the-blanks Articles with instructions and a fee schedule (including the fees for dissolution, restatement, change of the agent etc). You can also download the forms from the Internet under the address mentioned above. For successful download, you need the Acrobat Reader™ from Adobe®.

What must be filed:

Complete the fill-in-the-blanks forms and send the original and one copy to the Department of Financial Institutions. Enclose the filing fee. For expedited service (filing procedure will be completed the next business day), mark your documents "For Expedited Service" and provide an extra $25 for each item. Indicate on the back side of your Articles where the acknowledgement copy of the filed document should be sent.

Name requirements:

The corporate name must include the words "Corporation," "Incorporated," "Limited," or the abbreviation of one of those words.

For name availability, call the filing office prior to filing. A name can be reserved either by calling 608-261-9555 or by a written application. The application must include the name and address of the applicant and the name to be reserved. If the name is available, it will be reserved for 120 days. The reservation fee is $15 for the written application, $30 for the telephone application.

If your first choice is not available, you can provide a second choice name on the reverse side of your Articles.

Directors requirements:

Your corporation must have at least 3 directors. They don't have to be residents of Wisconsin.

Articles requirements:

The minimum requirements are as follows:
- corporate name
- the phrase: "The corporation is organized under Chapter 181 of the Wisconsin Statutes"
- name and address of the registered agent (street address of the agent's office is required, post office box address may be part of the address, but is sufficient alone)
- mailing address of the corporation's principal office (it may be located outside of Wisconsin)
- a statement whether the corporation will have members or not
- name, address, and signature of each incorporator
- name of the person who drafted the document (printed, typewritten or stamped in a legible manner)

Filing fees:

$35 filing fee payable to the Department of Financial Institutions, $16 standard recording fee payable to Register of Deeds (if you append additional pages to the form you have to pay $2 more recording fee for each additional page)

Reports:

You have to file an annual report within the calendar quarter of the anniversary of Incorporation.

Statute: Wisconsin Statutes, Chapter 181

TAXES:

Department of Revenue
P.O. Box 8906
Madison, WI 53708
Tel.: 608-266-2776
Website: http://www.dor.state.wi.us/

Automatic exemption: Yes

CHARITABLE SOLICITATION:

Department of Regulations and Licensing
P.O. Box 8935
Madison, WI 53708
Tel.: 608-266-0829

Statute: Wisconsin Statutes, Chapter 440, Subchapter 3

Exemption: None

Annual filing: Yes

Accept URS: No

WYOMING

INCORPORATION:

Secretary of State
State Capitol Building
Cheyenne, WY 82002
Tel.: 307-777-7311
Fax: 307-777-5339
or
Tel.: 307-777-7312
Website: soswy.state.wy.us/
email: Corporations@missc.state.wy.us

What they supply:

State provides fill-in-the-blanks form of Articles of Incorporation and of the "Consent to Appointment by Registered Agent" with instructions how to complete these forms.

What must be filed:

Complete the forms and file the original and one exact copy. The articles must be accompanied by the written consent to appointment executed by the registered agent. Enclose the filing fee.

Name requirements:

There are no special name requirements although your name may contain words like "corporation," "incorporated," or "company." It must be distinguishable from any other corporate name already on file and may not contain language that implies the corporation was organized for other purposes than those stated in the articles.

A name can be reserved for a fee of $30.

Directors requirements:

Your corporation must have at least 3 directors. They don't have to be residents of Wyoming.

Articles requirements:

Your articles must contain the following minimum:

- the corporate name
- a statement whether the corporation is a religious, a public benefit or a mutual benefit corporation
- the street address of your corporation's initial registered office and the name of the registered agent
- the name and address of each incorporator
- a statement whether your corporation shall have members
- provisions regarding the distribution of assets upon the dissolution of the corporation
- the date and signature of each incorporator

Don't forget to let your registered agent sign the "Consent to Appointment."

Filing fees:

$10, payable to the Secretary of State

Reports:

The annual report must be filed on the first day of the registration anniversary month. The secretary of State will send out forms two months prior to the due date.

Statute: Wyoming Statute, Section 17-6-102

TAXES:

Department of Revenue
Herschler Building
122 W. 25th Street
Cheyenne, WY 82002
Tel.: 307-777-5235
Website:http://revenue.state.wy.us/

Automatic Exemption: Yes

CHARITABLE SOLICITATION:

Secretary of State
Capitol Building
200 W. 24th St.
Cheyenne, WY 82002
Tel.: 307-777-7378

Statute: Wyoming Statutes 17-19-1501

Exemptions:

No current registration requirements for solicitation of charitable contributions

Annual filing: No

Accept URS: No

APPENDIX C
NONPROFIT
CORPORATE FORMS

_____
(date)

_____
_____
_____
_____

Dear Sir or Madam:

Please send me any and all forms, instructions, and statutes which are available without charge for forming a **domestic nonprofit corporation**.

Thank you,

_____

(date)

_____
_____
_____
_____

Dear Sir or Madam:

Please send me any and all forms, instructions, statutes, and other information necessary for registering and obtaining a tax exemption for a **domestic nonprofit corporation**.

Thank you,

_____
(date)

_____
_____
_____
_____

Dear Sir or Madam:

Please send me any and all forms, instructions, statutes, and other information on registration for charitable solicitation in this state for a **domestic nonprofit** corporation.

Thank you,

ARTICLES OF INCORPORATION

of

_____

A NONPROFIT CORPORATION

Articles of Incorporation of the undersigned, a majority of whom are citizens of the United States, desiring to form a Non-Profit Corporation under the Non-Profit Corporation Law of _____, do hereby certify:

    Article 1: The name of the corporation shall be:

    Article 2: The Place in this state where the principal office of the Corporation is to be initially located is the City of _____, _____ County.

    Article 3: Said corporation is organized exclusively for charitable, religious, educational, and scientific purposes, including, for such purposes, the making of distributions to organizations that qualify as exempt organizations under section 501(c)(3) of the Internal Revenue Code, or the corresponding section of any future tax code. The specific purpose of the corporation is to _____
_____
_____
_____.

    Article 4: The corporation shall have _____ directors. The initial directors' name(s) and address(es) is/are:

    Article 5: No part of the net earnings of the corporation shall inure to the benefit of or be distributable to its members, trustees, officers, or other private persons, except that the corporation shall be authorized and empowered to pay reasonable compensation for services rendered and to make payments and distributions in furtherance of the purposes set forth in Article 3 hereof. No substantial part of the activities of the corporation shall be the carrying on of propaganda, or otherwise attempting to influence legislation, and the corporation shall not participate in, or intervene in (including the publishing or distribution of statements), any political campaign on behalf of or in opposition to any candidate for public office. Notwithstanding any other provision of these articles, this corporation shall not, except to an insubstantial degree, engage in any activities or exercise any powers that are not in furtherance of the purposes of the corporation.

    Article 6: Upon the dissolution of the corporation, assets shall be distributed for one or more exempt purposes within the meaning of section 501(c)(3) of the Internal Revenue Code, or the corresponding section of any future federal tax code, or shall be distributed to the federal government, or to a state or local government, for a public purpose. Any such assets not so disposed shall be disposed of by a Court of Competent Jurisdiction of the county in which the principal office of the corporation is then located, exclusively for such purposes or to such organizations, as said Court shall determine, which are operated exclusively for such purposes.

Article 7: The registered agent and registered office of this corporation are:

Article 8: The corporation ☐ shall ☐ shall not have members. The classes, qualifications, rights and obligations of the members of the corporation (if any) are spelled out in the Bylaws of the corporation.

Article 9: The period of duration of the corporation is perpetual.

Article 10: Names and addresses of Incorporators:

Article 11:

In witness whereof, we have hereunto subscribed our names this _____ day of _____, 20_____.

_____   _____
Incorporator   Incorporator

_____   _____
Incorporator   Incorporator

The undersigned, being the registered (or statutory) agent listed in these Articles of Incorporation hereby accepts the position as such and agrees to act in such capacity. The undersigned further represents that he or she is familiar with the obligations of the position and agrees to comply with them.

_____
Registered Agent

ADDENDUM TO ARTICLES OF INCORPORATION
of

_____

A NONPROFIT CORPORATION

This Addendum to Articles of Incorporation of the above-named corporation is hereby made a part of said Articles of Incorporation as follows:

Article ___: The Place in this state where the principal office of the Corporation is to be initially located is the City of _____, _____ County.

Article ___: Said corporation is organized exclusively for charitable, religious, educational, and scientific purposes, including, for such purposes, the making of distributions to organizations that qualify as exempt organizations under section 501(c)(3) of the Internal Revenue Code, or the corresponding section of any future tax code.

Article ___: No part of the net earnings of the corporation shall inure to the benefit of or be distributable to its members, trustees, officers, or other private persons, except that the corporation shall be authorized and empowered to pay reasonable compensation for services rendered and to make payments and distributions in furtherance of the purposes set forth in Article___ of the Articles of the Incorporation. No substantial part of the activities of the corporation shall be the carrying on of propaganda, or otherwise attempting to influence legislation, and the corporation shall not participate in, or intervene in (including the publishing or distribution of statements), any political campaign on behalf of or in opposition to any candidate for public office. Notwithstanding any other provision of these articles, this corporation shall not, except to an insubstantial degree, engage in any activities or exercise any powers that are not in furtherance of the purposes of the corporation.

Article ___: Upon the dissolution of the corporation, assets shall be distributed for one or more exempt purposes within the meaning of section 501(c)(3) of the Internal Revenue Code, or the corresponding section of any future federal tax code, or shall be distributed to the federal government, or to a state or local government, for a public purpose. Any such assets not so disposed shall be disposed of by a Court of Competent Jurisdiction of the county in which the principal office of the corporation is then located, exclusively for such purposes or to such organizations, as said Court shall determine, which are operated exclusively for such purposes.

BYLAWS OF

A NOT-FOR-PROFIT CORPORATION

ARTICLE I - OFFICES

The principal office of the Corporation shall be located in the City of
_____ and the State of _____. The Corporation
may also maintain offices at such other places as the Board of Directors may, from time to
time, determine.

ARTICLE II - PURPOSE

Section 1 - Purpose. Said corporation is organized exclusively for charitable, religious,
educational, and scientific purposes, including, for such purposes, the making of distributions
to organizations that qualify as exempt organizations under section 501(c)(3) of the Internal
Revenue Code, or the corresponding section of any future tax code. The specific purpose of
the corporation is to _____

_____

_____

_____

_____

_____.

Section 2 - No private inurement. No part of the net earnings of the corporation shall inure
to the benefit of or be distributable to its members, trustees, officers, or other private persons,
except that the corporation shall be authorized and empowered to pay reasonable
compensation for services rendered and to make payments and distributions in furtherance of
the purposes set forth in Section 1 hereof.

Section 3 - No lobbying. No substantial part of the activities of the corporation shall be the
carrying on of propaganda, or otherwise attempting to influence legislation, and the
corporation shall not participate in, or intervene in (including the publishing or distribution of
statements) any political campaign on behalf of or in opposition to any candidate for public
office. Notwithstanding any other provision of these articles, this corporation shall not, except
to an insubstantial degree, engage in any activities or exercise any powers that are not in
furtherance of the purposes of the corporation

Section 4 - Dissolution. Upon the dissolution of the corporation, assets shall be distributed for
one or more exempt purposes within the meaning of section 501(c)(3) of the Internal
Revenue Code, or the corresponding section of any future federal tax code, or shall be
distributed to the federal government, or to a state or local government, for a public purpose.
Any such assets not so disposed shall be disposed of by a Court of Competent Jurisdiction of
the county in which the principal office of the corporation is then located, exclusively for such

purposes or to such organizations, as said Court shall determine, which are operated exclusively for such purposes.

Section 5 - Private Foundation. In the event that the Corporation fails to qualify as a public charity under federal tax law and is considered a private foundation, the corporation shall comply with the following: a) It will distribute its income for each tax year at such time and in such manner so that it will not become subject to the tax on undistributed taxable income imposed by section 4942 of the Internal Revenue Code, or corresponding provisions of any later federal tax laws; b) It will not engage in any act of self-dealing as defined in section 4941(d) of the Internal Revenue Code, or corresponding provisions of any later federal tax laws; c) It will not retain any excess business holdings as defined in section 4943(c) of the Internal Revenue Code, or corresponding provisions of any later federal tax laws; d) It will not make any investments in a manner that would subject it to tax under section 4944 of the Internal Revenue Code, or corresponding provisions of any later federal tax laws; and e) It will not make any taxable expenditures as defined in section 4945(d) of the Internal Revenue Code, or corresponding provisions of any later federal tax laws.

ARTICLE III - MEMBERS

Section 1 - Members. The corporation ☐ shall ☐ shall not have members.

Section 2 - Membership Provisions. If the corporation has members, the terms and conditions of membership shall be set out in an Addendum to these Bylaws.

ARTICLE IV - BOARD OF DIRECTORS

Section 1 - Number, Election and Term of Office. The number of the directors of the Corporation shall be _____. This number may be increased or decreased by the amendment of these bylaws by the Board but shall in no case be less than ____ director(s). The Board of Directors shall be elected each year. If this corporation has no members then the Board shall be elected by a majority of the votes of the then current Board. If the corporation has members then the Board shall be elected by the members at their annual meeting. Each director shall hold office until the next annual meeting, and until his successor is elected and qualified, or until his prior death, resignation, or removal.

Section 2 - Vacancies. Any vacancy in the Board shall be filled for the unexpired portion of the term by a majority vote of the remaining directors at any regular meeting or special meeting of the Board called for that purpose.

Section 3 - Duties and Powers. The Board shall be responsible for the control and management of the affairs, property, and interests of the Corporation and may exercise all powers of the Corporation, except as limited by statute.

Section 4 - Annual Meetings. An annual meeting of the Board shall be held on the ____ day of _____ each year unless rescheduled by the Board. The Board from time to time, may provide by resolution for the holding of other meetings of the Board, and may fix the time and place thereof.

Section 5 - Special Meetings. Special meetings of the Board shall be held whenever called by the President or by one of the directors, at such time and place as may be specified in the respective notice or waivers of notice thereof.

Section 6 - Notice and Waiver. Notice of any special meeting shall be given at least five days prior thereto by written notice delivered personally, by mail or by facsimile to each Director at his address. If mailed, such notice shall be deemed to be delivered when deposited in the United States Mail with postage prepaid. Any Director may waive notice of any meeting, either before, at, or after such meeting, by signing a waiver of notice. The attendance of a Director at a meeting shall constitute a waiver of notice of such meeting and a waiver of any and all objections to the place of such meeting, or the manner in which it has been called or convened, except when a Director states at the beginning of the meeting any objection to the transaction of business because the meeting is not lawfully called or convened.

Section 7 - Chairman. The Board may, at its discretion, elect a Chairman. At all meetings of the Board, the Chairman of the Board, if any and if present, shall preside. If there is no Chairman, or he or she is absent, then the President shall preside, and in his absence, a Chairman chosen by the directors shall preside.

Section 8 - Quorum and Adjournments. At all meetings of the Board, the presence of a majority of the entire Board shall be necessary and sufficient to constitute a quorum for the transaction of business, except as otherwise provided by law, by the Articles of Incorporation, or by these bylaws. A majority of the directors present at the time and place of any regular or special meeting, although less than a quorum, may adjourn the same from time to time without notice, until a quorum shall be present.

Section 9 - Board Action. At all meetings of the Board, each director present shall have one vote. Except as otherwise provided by Statute, the action of a majority of the directors present at any meeting at which a quorum is present shall be the act of the Board. Any action authorized, in writing, by all of the Directors entitled to vote thereon and filed with the minutes of the Corporation shall be the act of the Board with the same force and effect as if the same had been passed by unanimous vote at a duly called meeting of the Board. Any action taken by the Board may be taken without a meeting if agreed to in writing by all members before or after the action is taken and if a record of such action is filed in the minute book.

Section 10 - Telephone Meetings. Directors may participate in meetings of the Board through use of a telephone if such can be arranged so that all Board members can hear all other members. The use of a telephone for participation shall constitute presence in person.

Section 11 - Resignation and Removal. Any director may resign at any time by giving written notice to another Board member, the President or the Secretary of the Corporation. Unless otherwise specified in such written notice, such resignation shall take effect upon receipt thereof by the Board or by such officer, and the acceptance of such resignation shall not be necessary to make it effective. Any director may be removed for cause by action of the Board.

Section 12 - Compensation. No stated salary shall be paid to directors, as such for their services, but by resolution of the Board a fixed sum and/or expenses of attendance, if any, may be allowed for attendance at each regular or special meeting of the Board. Nothing herein contained shall be construed to preclude any director from serving the Corporation in any other capacity and receiving compensation therefor.

Section 13 - Liability. No director shall be liable for any debt, obligation or liability of the corporation.

ARTICLE V - OFFICERS

Section 1 - Number, Qualification, Election and Term. The officers of the Corporation shall consist of a President, a Secretary, a Treasurer, and such other officers, as the Board may from time to time deem advisable. Any officer may be, but is not required to be, a director of the Corporation. The officers of the Corporation shall be elected by the Board at the regular annual meeting of the Board. Each officer shall hold office until the annual meeting of the Board next succeeding his election, and until his successor shall have been elected and qualified, or until his death, resignation or removal.

Section 2 - Resignation and Removal. Any officer may resign at any time by giving written notice of such resignation to the President or the Secretary of the Corporation or to a member of the Board. Unless otherwise specified in such written notice, such resignation shall take effect upon receipt thereof by the Board member or by such officer, and the acceptance of such resignation shall not be necessary to make it effective. Any officer may be removed, either with or without cause, and a successor elected by a majority vote of the Board at any time.

Section 3 - Vacancies. A vacancy in any office may, at any time, be filled for the unexpired portion of the term by a majority vote of the Board.

Section 4 - Duties of Officers. Officers of the Corporation shall, unless otherwise provided by the Board, each have such powers and duties as generally pertain to their respective offices as well as such powers and duties as may from time to time be specifically decided by the Board. The President shall be the chief executive officer of the Corporation.

Section 5 - Compensation. The officers of the Corporation shall be entitled to such compensation as the Board shall from time to time determine.

Section 6 - Delegation of Duties. In the absence or disability of any Officer of the Corporation or for any other reason deemed sufficient by the Board of Directors, the Board may delegate his powers or duties to any other Officer or to any other Director.

Section 7 - Shares of Other Corporations. Whenever the Corporation is the holder of shares of any other Corporation, any right or power of the Corporation as such shareholder (including the attendance, acting and voting at shareholders' meetings and execution of waivers, consents, proxies or other instruments) may be exercised on behalf of the Corporation by the President, any Vice President, or such other person as the Board may authorize.

Section 8 - Liability. No officer shall be liable for any debt, obligation or liability of the corporation.

ARTICLE VI - COMMITTEES

Section 1 - Committees. The Board of Directors may, by resolution, designate an Executive Committee and one or more other committees. Such committees shall have such functions and may exercise such power of the Board of Directors as can be lawfully delegated, and to the extent provided in the resolution or resolutions creating such committee or committees. Meetings of committees may be held without notice at such time and at such place as shall from time to time be determined by the committees. The committees of the corporation shall keep regular minutes of their proceedings, and report these minutes to the Board of Directors when required.

ARTICLE VII - BOOKS, RECORDS AND REPORTS

Section 1 - Annual Report. The President of the Corporation shall cause to be prepared annual or other reports required by law and shall provide copies to the Board of Directors.

Section 2 - Permanent Records. The corporation shall keep current and correct records of the accounts, minutes of the meetings and proceedings and membership records (if any) of the corporation. Such records shall be kept at the registered office or the principal place of business of the corporation. Any such records shall be in written form or in a form capable of being converted into written form.

Section 3 - Inspection of Corporate Records. If this corporation has members, then those members shall have the right at any reasonable time, and on written demand stating the purpose thereof, to examine and make copies from the relevant books and records of accounts, minutes, and records of the Corporation.

ARTICLE VIII - FISCAL YEAR

Section 1 - Fiscal year. The fiscal year of the Corporation shall be the period selected by the Board of Directors as the tax year of the Corporation for federal income tax purposes.

ARTICLE IX - CORPORATE SEAL

Section 1 - Seal. The Board of Directors may adopt, use and modify a corporate seal. Failure to affix the seal to corporate documents shall not affect the validity of such document.

ARTICLE X - AMENDMENTS

Section 1 - Articles of Incorporation. The Articles of Incorporation may be amended by the Board of Directors unless this corporation has members, in which case they can be amended as provided by law.

Section 2 - Bylaws. These Bylaws may be amended by the Board of Directors

ARTICLE XI - INDEMNIFICATION

Section 1 - Indemnification. Any officer, director or employee of the Corporation shall be indemnified and held harmless to the full extent allowed by law.

Section 2 - Insurance. The corporation may but is not required to obtain insurance providing for indemnification of directors, officers and employees.

Certified to be the Bylaws of the corporation adopted by the Board of Directors on _____, 20____.

_____
Secretary

ADDENDUM TO BYLAWS OF

_____

A NONPROFIT CORPORATION

MEMBERS

Section 1 - Members. The corporation shall have one class of members and each member shall have one vote. The Corporation shall keep a list of all active members. Memberships shall not be transferable.

Section 2 - Admission and Termination. Any person may be admitted to membership in the corporation upon payment of such application fee and dues as shall be determined by the board of directors. A member may terminate his or her membership at any time by giving notice to an officer or director of the corporation. The Board of Directors may terminate a member who is delinquent in paying dues or who has acted contrary to the interests of the Corporation. Prior to termination of a member, the Corporation shall give said member 30 days written notice to pay the dues or to explain satisfactorily to the Board alleged to be contrary to the interests of the Corporation.

Section 3 - Annual Meetings. The annual meeting of the members of the Corporation shall be held each year on the _____ day of _____ at the principal office of the Corporation or at such other date and place as the Board may authorize, for the purpose of electing directors, and transacting such other business as may properly come before the meeting.

Section 4 - Special Meetings. Special meetings of the members may be called at any time by the Board, the President, or by the holders of twenty-five percent (25%) of the shares then outstanding and entitled to vote.

Section 5 - Notice of Meetings. Written or printed notice stating the place, day, and hour of the meeting and, in the case of a special meeting, the purpose of the meeting, shall be delivered personally or by mail not less than ten days, nor more than sixty days, before the date of the meeting. Notice shall be given to each Member of record entitled to vote at the meeting. If mailed, such notice shall be deemed to have been delivered when deposited in the United States Mail with postage paid and addressed to the Member at his address as it appears on the records of the Corporation.

Section 6 - Waiver of Notice. A written waiver of notice signed by a Member, whether before or after a meeting, shall be equivalent to the giving of such notice. Attendance of a Member at a meeting shall constitute a waiver of notice of such meeting, except when the Member attends for the express purpose of objecting, at the beginning of the meeting, to the transaction of any business because the meeting is not lawfully called or convened.

Section 7 - Quorum. Except as otherwise provided by Statute, or the Articles of Incorporation, at all meetings of Members of the Corporation, the presence at the commencement of such meetings in person or by proxy of a majority of the total membership of the Corporation entitled to vote, but in no event less than one-third of the Members entitled to vote at the meeting, shall constitute a quorum for the transaction of any business. If any Member leaves after the commencement of a meeting, this shall have no effect on the existence of a quorum, after a quorum has been established at such meeting.

Despite the absence of a quorum at any annual or special meeting of members, the members, by a majority of the votes cast by those entitled to vote thereon, may adjourn the meeting. At any such adjourned meeting at which a quorum is present, any business may be transacted at the meeting as originally called as if a quorum had been present.

Section 8 - Voting. Except as otherwise provided by Statute or by the Articles of Incorporation, any corporate action, other than the election of directors, to be taken by vote of the members, shall be authorized by a majority of votes cast at a meeting of Members.

Except as otherwise provided by Statute or by the Articles of Incorporation, at each meeting of Members, active Member of the Corporation shall be entitled to one vote.

Each Member entitled to vote may do so by proxy; provided, however, that the instrument authorizing such proxy to act shall have been executed in writing by the member himself. No proxy shall be valid after the expiration of eleven months from the date of its execution, unless the person executing it shall have specified therein, the length of time it is to continue in force. Such instrument shall be exhibited to the Secretary at the meeting and shall be filed with the records of the corporation.

Any resolution in writing, signed by all of the Members entitled to vote thereon, shall be and constitute action by such Members to the effect therein expressed, with the same force and effect as if the same had been duly passed by unanimous vote at a duly called meeting of Members and such resolution so signed shall be inserted in the Minute Book of the Corporation under its proper date.

Form **SS-4**	**Application for Employer Identification Number**	EIN

Form **SS-4**

(Rev. February 1998)

Department of the Treasury
Internal Revenue Service

Application for Employer Identification Number

(For use by employers, corporations, partnerships, trusts, estates, churches, government agencies, certain individuals, and others. See instructions.)

▶ Keep a copy for your records.

EIN

OMB No. 1545-0003

Please type or print clearly.

1 Name of applicant (legal name) (see instructions)

2 Trade name of business (if different from name on line 1) | **3** Executor, trustee, "care of" name

4a Mailing address (street address) (room, apt., or suite no.) | **5a** Business address (if different from address on lines 4a and 4b)

4b City, state, and ZIP code | **5b** City, state, and ZIP code

6 County and state where principal business is located

7 Name of principal officer, general partner, grantor, owner, or trustor—SSN or ITIN may be required (see instructions) ▶

8a Type of entity (Check only one box.) (see instructions)

Caution: *If applicant is a limited liability company, see the instructions for line 8a.*

☐ Sole proprietor (SSN) _____
☐ Partnership   ☐ Personal service corp.
☐ REMIC   ☐ National Guard
☐ State/local government ☐ Farmers' cooperative
☐ Church or church-controlled organization
☐ Other nonprofit organization (specify) ▶ _____
☐ Other (specify) ▶

☐ Estate (SSN of decedent) _____
☐ Plan administrator (SSN) _____
☐ Other corporation (specify) ▶ _____
☐ Trust
☐ Federal government/military
(enter GEN if applicable) _____

8b If a corporation, name the state or foreign country (if applicable) where incorporated | State | Foreign country

9 Reason for applying (Check only one box.) (see instructions)
☐ Started new business (specify type) ▶_____
☐ Hired employees (Check the box and see line 12.)
☐ Created a pension plan (specify type) ▶
☐ Banking purpose (specify purpose) ▶_____
☐ Changed type of organization (specify new type) ▶_____
☐ Purchased going business
☐ Created a trust (specify type) ▶_____
☐ Other (specify) ▶

10 Date business started or acquired (month, day, year) (see instructions) | **11** Closing month of accounting year (see instructions)

12 First date wages or annuities were paid or will be paid (month, day, year). **Note:** *If applicant is a withholding agent, enter date income will first be paid to nonresident alien. (month, day, year)* . . . . ▶

13 Highest number of employees expected in the next 12 months. **Note:** *If the applicant does not expect to have any employees during the period, enter -0-. (see instructions)* . . . . ▶ | Nonagricultural | Agricultural | Household

14 Principal activity (see instructions) ▶

15 Is the principal business activity manufacturing? . . . . ☐ Yes ☐ No
If "Yes," principal product and raw material used ▶

16 To whom are most of the products or services sold? Please check one box.   ☐ Business (wholesale)
☐ Public (retail)   ☐ Other (specify) ▶   ☐ N/A

17a Has the applicant ever applied for an employer identification number for this or any other business? . . . . ☐ Yes ☐ No
Note: *If "Yes," please complete lines 17b and 17c.*

17b If you checked "Yes" on line 17a, give applicant's legal name and trade name shown on prior application, if different from line 1 or 2 above.
Legal name ▶   Trade name ▶

17c Approximate date when and city and state where the application was filed. Enter previous employer identification number if known.
Approximate date when filed (mo., day, year) | City and state where filed | Previous EIN

Under penalties of perjury, I declare that I have examined this application, and to the best of my knowledge and belief, it is true, correct, and complete. | Business telephone number (include area code)

Fax telephone number (include area code)

Name and title (Please type or print clearly.) ▶

Signature ▶   Date ▶

Note: *Do not write below this line. For official use only.*

Please leave blank ▶ | Geo. | Ind. | Class | Size | Reason for applying

For Paperwork Reduction Act Notice, see page 4. | Cat. No. 16055N | Form **SS-4** (Rev. 2-98)

153

General Instructions

Section references are to the Internal Revenue Code unless otherwise noted.

Purpose of Form

Use Form SS-4 to apply for an employer identification number (EIN). An EIN is a nine-digit number (for example, 12-3456789) assigned to sole proprietors, corporations, partnerships, estates, trusts, and other entities for tax filing and reporting purposes. The information you provide on this form will establish your business tax account.

Caution: *An EIN is for use in connection with your business activities only. Do **NOT** use your EIN in place of your social security number (SSN).*

Who Must File

You must file this form if you have not been assigned an EIN before and:

- You pay wages to one or more employees including household employees.

- You are required to have an EIN to use on any return, statement, or other document, even if you are not an employer.

- You are a withholding agent required to withhold taxes on income, other than wages, paid to a nonresident alien (individual, corporation, partnership, etc.). A withholding agent may be an agent, broker, fiduciary, manager, tenant, or spouse, and is required to file **Form 1042,** Annual Withholding Tax Return for U.S. Source Income of Foreign Persons.

- You file **Schedule C,** Profit or Loss From Business, **Schedule C-EZ,** Net Profit From Business, or **Schedule F,** Profit or Loss From Farming, of **Form 1040,** U.S. Individual Income Tax Return, **and** have a Keogh plan or are required to file excise, employment, or alcohol, tobacco, or firearms returns.

The following must use EINs even if they do not have any employees:

- State and local agencies who serve as tax reporting agents for public assistance recipients, under Rev. Proc. 80-4, 1980-1 C.B. 581, should obtain a separate EIN for this reporting. See **Household employer** on page 3.
- Trusts, except the following:

   1. Certain grantor-owned trusts. (See the **Instructions for Form 1041.**)

   2. Individual Retirement Arrangement (IRA) trusts, unless the trust has to file **Form 990-T,** Exempt Organization Business Income Tax Return. (See the **Instructions for Form 990-T.**)

- Estates
- Partnerships
- REMICs (real estate mortgage investment conduits) (See the **Instructions for Form 1066,** U.S. Real Estate Mortgage Investment Conduit Income Tax Return.)
- Corporations
- Nonprofit organizations (churches, clubs, etc.)
- Farmers' cooperatives
- Plan administrators (A plan administrator is the person or group of persons specified as the administrator by the instrument under which the plan is operated.)

When To Apply for a New EIN

New Business. If you become the new owner of an existing business, **do not** use the EIN of the former owner. IF YOU ALREADY HAVE AN EIN, USE THAT NUMBER. If you do not have an EIN, apply for one on this form. If you become the "owner" of a corporation by acquiring its stock, use the corporation's EIN.

Changes in Organization or Ownership. If you already have an EIN, you may need to get a new one if either the organization or ownership of your business changes. If you incorporate a sole proprietorship or form a partnership, you must get a new EIN. However, **do not** apply for a new EIN if:

- You change only the name of your business,
- You elected on **Form 8832,** Entity Classification Election, to change the way the entity is taxed, or
- A partnership terminates because at least 50% of the total interests in partnership capital and profits were sold or exchanged within a 12-month period. (See Regulations section 301.6109-1(d)(2)(iii).) The EIN for the terminated partnership should continue to be used. This rule applies to terminations occurring after May 8, 1997. If the termination took place after May 8, 1996, and before May 9, 1997, a new EIN must be obtained for the new partnership unless the partnership and its partners are consistent in using the old EIN.

Note: *If you are electing to be an "S corporation," be sure you file **Form 2553,** Election by a Small Business Corporation.*

File Only One Form SS-4. File only one Form SS-4, regardless of the number of businesses operated or trade names under which a business operates. However, each corporation in an affiliated group must file a separate application.

EIN Applied for, But Not Received. If you do not have an EIN by the time a return is due, write "Applied for" and the date you applied in the space shown for the number. **Do not** show your social security number (SSN) as an EIN on returns.

If you do not have an EIN by the time a tax deposit is due, send your payment to the Internal Revenue Service Center for your filing area. (See **Where To Apply** below.) Make your check or money order payable to Internal Revenue Service and show your name (as shown on Form SS-4), address, type of tax, period covered, and date you applied for an EIN. Send an explanation with the deposit.

For more information about EINs, see **Pub. 583,** Starting a Business and Keeping Records, and **Pub. 1635,** Understanding your EIN.

How To Apply

You can apply for an EIN either by mail or by telephone. You can get an EIN immediately by calling the Tele-TIN number for the service center for your state, or you can send the completed Form SS-4 directly to the service center to receive your EIN by mail.

Application by Tele-TIN. Under the Tele-TIN program, you can receive your EIN by telephone and use it immediately to file a return or make a payment. To receive an EIN by telephone, complete Form SS-4, then call the Tele-TIN number listed for your state under **Where To Apply.** The person making the call must be authorized to sign the form. (See **Signature** on page 4.)

An IRS representative will use the information from the Form SS-4 to establish your account and assign you an EIN. Write the number you are given on the upper right corner of the form and sign and date it.

*Mail or fax (facsimile) the signed SS-4 **within 24 hours** to the Tele-TIN Unit at the service center address for your state.* The IRS representative will give you the fax number. The fax numbers are also listed in Pub. 1635.

Taxpayer representatives can receive their client's EIN by telephone if they first send a fax of a completed **Form 2848,** Power of Attorney and Declaration of Representative, or **Form 8821,** Tax Information Authorization, to the Tele-TIN unit. The Form 2848 or Form 8821 will be used solely to release the EIN to the representative authorized on the form.

Application by Mail. Complete Form SS-4 at least 4 to 5 weeks before you will need an EIN. Sign and date the application and mail it to the service center address for your state. You will receive your EIN in the mail in approximately 4 weeks.

Where To Apply

The Tele-TIN numbers listed below will involve a long-distance charge to callers outside of the local calling area and can be used only to apply for an EIN. THE NUMBERS MAY CHANGE WITHOUT NOTICE. Call 1-800-829-1040 to verify a number or to ask about the status of an application by mail.

If your principal business, office or agency, or legal residence in the case of an individual, is located in:	Call the Tele-TIN number shown or file with the Internal Revenue Service Center at:
Florida, Georgia, South Carolina	Attn: Entity Control Atlanta, GA 39901 770-455-2360
New Jersey, New York City and counties of Nassau, Rockland, Suffolk, and Westchester	Attn: Entity Control Holtsville, NY 00501 516-447-4955
New York (all other counties), Connecticut, Maine, Massachusetts, New Hampshire, Rhode Island, Vermont	Attn: Entity Control Andover, MA 05501 978-474-9717
Illinois, Iowa, Minnesota, Missouri, Wisconsin	Attn: Entity Control Stop 6800 2306 E. Bannister Rd. Kansas City, MO 64999 816-926-5999
Delaware, District of Columbia, Maryland, Pennsylvania, Virginia	Attn: Entity Control Philadelphia, PA 19255 215-516-6999
Indiana, Kentucky, Michigan, Ohio, West Virginia	Attn: Entity Control Cincinnati, OH 45999 606-292-5467

154

Kansas, New Mexico, Oklahoma, Texas	Attn: Entity Control Austin, TX 73301 512-460-7843
Alaska, Arizona, California (counties of Alpine, Amador, Butte, Calaveras, Colusa, Contra Costa, Del Norte, El Dorado, Glenn, Humboldt, Lake, Lassen, Marin, Mendocino, Modoc, Napa, Nevada, Placer, Plumas, Sacramento, San Joaquin, Shasta, Sierra, Siskiyou, Solano, Sonoma, Sutter, Tehama, Trinity, Yolo, and Yuba), Colorado, Idaho, Montana, Nebraska, Nevada, North Dakota, Oregon, South Dakota, Utah, Washington, Wyoming	Attn: Entity Control Mail Stop 6271 P.O. Box 9941 Ogden, UT 84201 801-620-7645
California (all other counties), Hawaii	Attn: Entity Control Fresno, CA 93888 209-452-4010
Alabama, Arkansas, Louisiana, Mississippi, North Carolina, Tennessee	Attn: Entity Control Memphis, TN 37501 901-546-3920
If you have no legal residence, principal place of business, or principal office or agency in any state	Attn: Entity Control Philadelphia, PA 19255 215-516-6999

Specific Instructions

The instructions that follow are for those items that are not self-explanatory. Enter N/A (nonapplicable) on the lines that do not apply.

Line 1. Enter the legal name of the entity applying for the EIN exactly as it appears on the social security card, charter, or other applicable legal document.

Individuals. Enter your first name, middle initial, and last name. If you are a sole proprietor, enter your individual name, not your business name. Enter your business name on line 2. Do not use abbreviations or nicknames on line 1.

Trusts. Enter the name of the trust.

Estate of a decedent. Enter the name of the estate.

Partnerships. Enter the legal name of the partnership as it appears in the partnership agreement. **Do not** list the names of the partners on line 1. See the specific instructions for line 7.

Corporations. Enter the corporate name as it appears in the corporation charter or other legal document creating it.

Plan administrators. Enter the name of the plan administrator. A plan administrator who already has an EIN should use that number.

Line 2. Enter the trade name of the business if different from the legal name. The trade name is the "doing business as" name.

Note: *Use the full legal name on line 1 on all tax returns filed for the entity. However, if you enter a trade name on line 2 and choose to use the trade name instead of the legal name, enter the trade name on all returns you file. To prevent processing delays and errors, always use either the legal name only or the trade name only on all tax returns.*

Line 3. Trusts enter the name of the trustee. Estates enter the name of the executor, administrator, or other fiduciary. If the entity applying has a designated person to receive tax information, enter that person's name as the "care of" person. Print or type the first name, middle initial, and last name.

Line 7. Enter the first name, middle initial, last name, and SSN of a principal officer if the business is a corporation; of a general partner if a partnership; of the owner of a single member entity that is disregarded as an entity separate from its owner; or of a grantor, owner, or trustor if a trust. If the person in question is an alien individual with a previously assigned individual taxpayer identification number (ITIN), enter the ITIN in the space provided, instead of an SSN. You are not required to enter an SSN or ITIN if the reason you are applying for an EIN is to make an entity classification election (see Regulations section 301.7701-1 through 301.7701-3), and you are a nonresident alien with no effectively connected income from sources within the United States.

Line 8a. Check the box that best describes the type of entity applying for the EIN. If you are an alien individual with an ITIN previously assigned to you, enter the ITIN in place of a requested SSN.

Caution: *This is not an election for a tax classification of an entity. See "Limited liability company" below.*

If not specifically mentioned, check the "Other" box, enter the type of entity and the type of return that will be filed (for example, common trust fund, Form 1065). Do not enter N/A. If you are an alien individual applying for an EIN, see the **Line 7** instructions above.

Sole proprietor. Check this box if you file Schedule C, C-EZ, or F (Form 1040) and have a Keogh plan, or are required to file excise, employment, or alcohol, tobacco, or firearms returns, or are a payer of gambling

winnings. Enter your SSN (or ITIN) in the space provided. If you are a nonresident alien with no effectively connected income from sources within the United States, you do not need to enter an SSN or ITIN.

REMIC. Check this box if the entity has elected to be treated as a real estate mortgage investment conduit (REMIC). See the **Instructions for Form 1066** for more information.

Other nonprofit organization. Check this box if the nonprofit organization is other than a church or church-controlled organization and specify the type of nonprofit organization (for example, an educational organization).

If the organization also seeks tax-exempt status, you must file either **Package 1023,** Application for Recognition of Exemption, or **Package 1024,** Application for Recognition of Exemption Under Section 501(a). Get **Pub. 557,** Tax Exempt Status for Your Organization, for more information.

Group exemption number (GEN). If the organization is covered by a group exemption letter, enter the four-digit GEN. (Do not confuse the GEN with the nine-digit EIN.) If you do not know the GEN, contact the parent organization. Get Pub. 557 for more information about group exemption numbers.

Withholding agent. If you are a withholding agent required to file Form 1042, check the "Other" box and enter "Withholding agent."

Personal service corporation. Check this box if the entity is a personal service corporation. An entity is a personal service corporation for a tax year only if:

● The principal activity of the entity during the testing period (prior tax year) for the tax year is the performance of personal services substantially by employee-owners, and

● The employee-owners own at least 10% of the fair market value of the outstanding stock in the entity on the last day of the testing period.

Personal services include performance of services in such fields as health, law, accounting, or consulting. For more information about personal service corporations, see the **Instructions for Form 1120,** U.S. Corporation Income Tax Return, and **Pub. 542,** Corporations.

Limited liability company (LLC). See the definition of limited liability company in the **Instructions for Form 1065.** An LLC with two or more members can be a partnership or an association taxable as a corporation. An LLC with a single owner can be an association taxable as a corporation or an entity disregarded as an entity separate from its owner. See Form 8832 for more details.

● If the entity is classified as a partnership for Federal income tax purposes, check the "partnership" box.

● If the entity is classified as a corporation for Federal income tax purposes, mark the "Other corporation" box and write "limited liability co." in the space provided.

● If the entity is disregarded as an entity separate from its owner, check the "Other" box and write in "disregarded entity" in the space provided.

Plan administrator. If the plan administrator is an individual, enter the plan administrator's SSN in the space provided.

Other corporation. This box is for any corporation other than a personal service corporation. If you check this box, enter the type of corporation (such as insurance company) in the space provided.

Household employer. If you are an individual, check the "Other" box and enter "Household employer" and your SSN. If you are a state or local agency serving as a tax reporting agent for public assistance recipients who become household employers, check the "Other" box and enter "Household employer agent." If you are a trust that qualifies as a household employer, you do not need a separate EIN for reporting tax information relating to household employees; use the EIN of the trust.

QSSS. For a qualified subchapter S subsidiary (QSSS) check the "Other" box and specify "QSSS."

Line 9. Check only **one** box. Do not enter N/A.

Started new business. Check this box if you are starting a new business that requires an EIN. If you check this box, enter the type of business being started. **Do not** apply if you already have an EIN and are only adding another place of business.

Hired employees. Check this box if the existing business is requesting an EIN because it has hired or is hiring employees and is therefore required to file employment tax returns. **Do not** apply if you already have an EIN and are only hiring employees. For information on the applicable employment taxes for family members, see **Circular E,** Employer's Tax Guide (Publication 15).

Created a pension plan. Check this box if you have created a pension plan and need this number for reporting purposes. Also, enter the type of plan created.

Note: *Check this box if you are applying for a trust EIN when a new pension plan is established.*

Banking purpose. Check this box if you are requesting an EIN for banking purposes only, and enter the banking purpose (for example, a bowling league for depositing dues or an investment club for dividend and interest reporting).

Changed type of organization. Check this box if the business is changing its type of organization, for example, if the business was a sole proprietorship and has been incorporated or has become a partnership. If you check this box, specify in the space provided the type of change made, for example, "from sole proprietorship to partnership."

Purchased going business. Check this box if you purchased an existing business. **Do not** use the former owner's EIN. **Do not** apply for a new EIN if you already have one. Use your own EIN.

Created a trust. Check this box if you created a trust, and enter the type of trust created. For example, indicate if the trust is a nonexempt charitable trust or a split-interest trust.

Note: *Do not check this box if you are applying for a trust EIN when a new pension plan is established. Check "Created a pension plan."*

Exception. Do **not** file this form for certain grantor-type trusts. The trustee does not need an EIN for the trust if the trustee furnishes the name and TIN of the grantor/owner and the address of the trust to all payors. See the Instructions for Form 1041 for more information.

Other (specify). Check this box if you are requesting an EIN for any reason other than those for which there are checkboxes, and enter the reason.

Line 10. If you are starting a new business, enter the starting date of the business. If the business you acquired is already operating, enter the date you acquired the business. Trusts should enter the date the trust was legally created. Estates should enter the date of death of the decedent whose name appears on line 1 or the date when the estate was legally funded.

Line 11. Enter the last month of your accounting year or tax year. An accounting or tax year is usually 12 consecutive months, either a calendar year or a fiscal year (including a period of 52 or 53 weeks). A calendar year is 12 consecutive months ending on December 31. A fiscal year is either 12 consecutive months ending on the last day of any month other than December or a 52-53 week year. For more information on accounting periods, see **Pub. 538,** Accounting Periods and Methods.

Individuals. Your tax year generally will be a calendar year.

Partnerships. Partnerships generally must adopt one of the following tax years:
● The tax year of the majority of its partners,
● The tax year common to all of its principal partners,
● The tax year that results in the least aggregate deferral of income, or
● In certain cases, some other tax year.
See the **Instructions for Form 1065,** U.S. Partnership Return of Income, for more information.

REMIC. REMICs must have a calendar year as their tax year.

Personal service corporations. A personal service corporation generally must adopt a calendar year unless:
● It can establish a business purpose for having a different tax year, or
● It elects under section 444 to have a tax year other than a calendar year.

Trusts. Generally, a trust must adopt a calendar year except for the following:
● Tax-exempt trusts,
● Charitable trusts, and
● Grantor-owned trusts.

Line 12. If the business has or will have employees, enter the date on which the business began or will begin to pay wages. If the business does not plan to have employees, enter N/A.

Withholding agent. Enter the date you began or will begin to pay income to a nonresident alien. This also applies to individuals who are required to file Form 1042 to report alimony paid to a nonresident alien.

Line 13. For a definition of agricultural labor (farmwork), see **Circular A,** Agricultural Employer's Tax Guide (Publication 51).

Line 14. Generally, enter the exact type of business being operated (for example, advertising agency, farm, food or beverage establishment, labor union, real estate agency, steam laundry, rental of coin-operated vending machine, or investment club). Also state if the business will involve the sale or distribution of alcoholic beverages.

Governmental. Enter the type of organization (state, county, school district, municipality, etc.).

Nonprofit organization (other than governmental). Enter whether organized for religious, educational, or humane purposes, and the principal activity (for example, religious organization—hospital, charitable).

Mining and quarrying. Specify the process and the principal product (for example, mining bituminous coal, contract drilling for oil, or quarrying dimension stone).

Contract construction. Specify whether general contracting or special trade contracting. Also, show the type of work normally performed (for example, general contractor for residential buildings or electrical subcontractor).

Food or beverage establishments. Specify the type of establishment and state whether you employ workers who receive tips (for example, lounge—yes).

Trade. Specify the type of sales and the principal line of goods sold (for example, wholesale dairy products, manufacturer's representative for mining machinery, or retail hardware).

Manufacturing. Specify the type of establishment operated (for example, sawmill or vegetable cannery).

Signature. The application must be signed by (a) the individual, if the applicant is an individual, (b) the president, vice president, or other principal officer, if the applicant is a corporation, (c) a responsible and duly authorized member or officer having knowledge of its affairs, if the applicant is a partnership or other unincorporated organization, or (d) the fiduciary, if the applicant is a trust or an estate.

How To Get Forms and Publications

Phone. You can order forms, instructions, and publications by phone. Just call 1-800-TAX-FORM (1-800-829-3676). You should receive your order or notification of its status within 7 to 15 workdays.

Personal computer. With your personal computer and modem, you can get the forms and information you need using:
● IRS's Internet Web Site at **www.irs.ustreas.gov**
● Telnet at **iris.irs.ustreas.gov**
● File Transfer Protocol at **ftp.irs.ustreas.gov**

You can also dial direct (by modem) to the Internal Revenue Information Services (IRIS) at 703-321-8020. IRIS is an on-line information service on FedWorld.

For small businesses, return preparers, or others who may frequently need tax forms or publications, a CD-ROM containing over 2,000 tax products (including many prior year forms) can be purchased from the Government Printing Office.

CD-ROM. To order the CD-ROM call the Superintendent of Documents at 202-512-1800 or connect to **www.access.gpo.gov/su_docs**

The time needed to complete and file this form will vary depending on individual circumstances. The estimated average time is:

Recordkeeping	7 min.
Learning about the law or the form	19 min.
Preparing the form	45 min.
Copying, assembling, and sending the form to the IRS . .	20 min.

If you have comments concerning the accuracy of these time estimates or suggestions for making this form simpler, we would be happy to hear from you. You can write to the Tax Forms Committee, Western Area Distribution Center, Rancho Cordova, CA 95743-0001. **Do not** send this form to this address. Instead, see **Where To Apply** on page 2.

Form **8718**
(Rev. January 1998)
Department of the Treasury
Internal Revenue Service

User Fee for Exempt Organization Determination Letter Request

► Attach this form to determination letter application.
(Form 8718 is NOT a determination letter application.)

For IRS Use Only

Control number _____

Amount paid _____

User fee screener

1 Name of organization	2 Employer Identification Number

Caution: *Do not attach Form 8718 to an application for a pension plan determination letter. Use Form 8717 instead.*

3 Type of request   **Fee**

a ☐ Initial request for a determination letter for:
- An exempt organization that has had annual gross receipts averaging not more than $10,000 during the preceding 4 years, or
- A new organization that anticipates gross receipts averaging not more than $10,000 during its first 4 years ► $150

Note: *If you checked box 3a, you must complete the Certification below.*

Certification

I certify that the annual gross receipts of ....
name of organization

have averaged (or are expected to average) not more than $10,000 during the preceding 4 (or the first 4) years of operation.

Signature ►   Title ►

b ☐ Initial request for a determination letter for:
- An exempt organization that has had annual gross receipts averaging more than $10,000 during the preceding 4 years, or
- A new organization that anticipates gross receipts averaging more than $10,000 during its first 4 years . ► $500

c ☐ Group exemption letters . . . . ► $500

Instructions

The law requires payment of a user fee with each application for a determination letter. The user fees are listed on line 3 above. For more information, see Rev. Proc. 98-8, 1998-1, I.R.B. 225.

Check the box on line 3 for the type of application you are submitting. If you check box 3a, you must complete and sign the certification statement that appears under line 3a.

Attach to Form 8718 a check or money order payable to the Internal Revenue Service for the full amount of the user fee. If you do not include the full amount, your application will be returned. Attach Form 8718 to your determination letter application.

Send the determination letter application and Form 8718 to:

Internal Revenue Service
P.O. Box 192
Covington, KY 41012-0192

If you are using express mail or a delivery service, send the application and Form 8718 to:

Internal Revenue Service
201 West Rivercenter Blvd.
Attn: Extracting Stop 312
Covington, KY 41011

Attach Check or Money Order Here

Cat. No. 64728Z

⊛ *Printed on recycled paper*

Form **8718** (Rev. 1-98)

*U.S. Government Printing Office: 1998 - 432-190/60336

WAIVER OF NOTICE

OF THE ORGANIZATION MEETING

OF

_____

We, the undersigned incorporators named in the articles or certificate of incorporation of the above-named corporation, hereby agree and consent that the organization meeting of the corporation be held on the date and time and place stated below and hereby waive all notice of such meeting and of any adjournment thereof.

Place of meeting: _____

Date of Meeting: _____

Time of meeting: _____

Dated: _____

_____
Incorporator

_____
Incorporator

_____
Incorporator

MINUTES IF THE ORGANIZATIONAL MEETING OF

INCORPORATORS AND DIRECTORS OF

_____

The organization meeting of the above corporation was held on _____ _____, 20_____ at _____ _____ at _____ o'clock ___M.

The following persons were present:

_____   _____
_____   _____
_____   _____

The Waiver of Notice of this meeting was signed by all directors and incorporators named in the Articles of Incorporation and filed in the minute book.

The meeting was called to order by _____ an Incorporator named in the Articles of Incorporation. _____ was nominated and elected Chairman and acted as such until relieved by the president. _____ was nominated and elected temporary secretary, and acted as such until relieved by the permanent secretary.

A copy of the Articles of Incorporation which was filed with the Secretary of State of the State of _____ on _____, 20____ was examined by the Directors and Incorporators and filed in the minute book.

The election of officers for the coming year was then held and the following were duly nominated and elected by the Board of Directors to be the officers of the corporation, to serve until such time as their successors are elected and qualified:

President: _____
Vice President: _____
Secretary: _____
Treasurer: _____

The proposed Bylaws for the corporation were then presented to the meeting and discussed. Upon motion duly made, seconded and carried, the Bylaws were adopted and added to the minute book.

A corporate seal for the corporation was then presented to the meeting and upon motion duly made, seconded, and carried, it was adopted as the seal of the corporation. An impression thereof was then made in the margin of these minutes.

The necessity of opening a bank account was then discussed and upon motion duly made, seconded, and carried, the following resolution was adopted:

RESOLVED that the corporation open bank accounts with _____ _____ and that the officers of the corporation are authorized to take such action as is necessary to open such accounts; that the bank's printed form of resolution is hereby adopted and incorporated into these minutes by reference and shall be placed in the minute book; that any _____ of the following persons shall have signature authority over the account:

_____   _____

_____   _____

_____   _____

The tax status of the corporation was then discussed and it was moved, seconded and carried that the officers of the corporation take the necessary action to:

1.   Obtain an employer tax number by filing form SS-4,

2.   Apply for exemption from taxation under IRC § 501(c)(   )

The expenses of organizing the corporation were then discussed and it was moved, seconded, and carried that the corporation pay in full from the corporate funds the expenses and reimburse any advances made by the incorporators upon proof of payment.

The Directors named in the Articles of Incorporation then tendered their resignations, effective upon the adjournment of this meeting. Upon motion duly made, seconded, and carried, the following named persons were elected as Directors of the corporation, each to hold office until the next election of Directors, and until a successor of each shall have been elected and qualified.

_____

_____

_____

_____

There being no further business before the meeting, on motion duly made, seconded, and carried, the meeting adjourned.

DATED: _____

_____
President

_____
Secretary

RESOLUTION TO REIMBURSE EXPENSES

OF

_____

A _____ CORPORATION

RESOLVED that the corporation shall reimburse the following parties for the organizational expenses of the organizers of this corporation and that the corporation shall amortize these expenses as allowed by IRS regulations.

Name	Expense	Amount
_____	_____	$_____
_____	_____	$_____
_____	_____	$_____
_____	_____	$_____
_____	_____	$_____

Date:_____

_____

_____

_____

_____

BANKING RESOLUTION OF

_____

The undersigned, being the corporate secretary of the above corporation, hereby certifies that on the _____ day of _____, 20___ the Board of Directors of the corporation adopted the following resolution:

RESOLVED that the corporation open bank accounts with _____ _____ and that the officers of the corporation are authorized to take such action as is necessary to open such accounts; that the bank's printed form of resolution is hereby adopted and incorporated into these minutes by reference and shall be placed in the minute book; and that any _____ of the following persons shall have signature authority over the account:

_____   _____

_____   _____

and that said resolution has not been modified or rescinded.

Date: _____

_____
Corporate Secretary

(Seal)

WAIVER OF NOTICE OF THE ANNUAL MEETING OF
THE BOARD OF DIRECTORS OF

_____

The undersigned, being all the Directors of the Corporation, hereby agree and consent that an annual meeting of the Board of Directors of the Corporation be held on the _____ day of _____, 20___ at ___ o'clock __M. at _____ _____ and do hereby waive all notice whatsoever of such meeting and of any adjournment or adjournments thereof.

We do further agree and consent that any and all lawful business may be transacted at such meeting or at any adjournment or adjournments thereof as may be deemed advisable by the Directors present. Any business transacted at such meeting or at any adjournment or adjournments thereof shall be as valid and legal as if such meeting or adjourned meeting were held after notice.

Date: _____

_____
Director

_____
Director

_____
Director

_____
Director

MINUTES OF THE ANNUAL MEETING OF
THE BOARD OF DIRECTORS OF

_____

The annual meeting of the Board of Directors of the Corporation was held on the date and at the time and place set forth in the written waiver of notice signed by the Directors, and attached to the minutes of this meeting.

The following were present, being all the directors of the Corporation:

_____   _____

_____   _____

The meeting was called to order and it was moved, seconded and unanimously carried that _____ act as Chairman and that _____ _____ act as Secretary.

The minutes of the last meeting of the Board of Directors which was held on _____, 20___ were read and approved by the Board.

Upon motion duly made, seconded and carried, the following were elected officers for the following year and until their successors are elected and qualify:

President:
Vice President:
Secretary
Treasurer:

There being no further business to come before the meeting, upon motion duly made, seconded and unanimously carried, it was adjourned.

_____
Secretary

Directors:

_____

_____

_____

_____

WAIVER OF NOTICE OF SPECIAL MEETING OF
THE BOARD OF DIRECTORS OF

_____

The undersigned, being all the Directors of the Corporation, hereby agree and consent that a special meeting of the Board of Directors of the Corporation be held on the _____ day of _____, 20___ at ___ o'clock __M. at _____ _____ and do hereby waive all notice whatsoever of such meeting and of any adjournment or adjournments thereof.

The purpose of the meeting is:

We do further agree and consent that any and all lawful business may be transacted at such meeting or at any adjournment or adjournments thereof as may be deemed advisable by the Directors present. Any business transacted at such meeting or at any adjournment or adjournments thereof shall be as valid and legal as if such meeting or adjourned meeting were held after notice.

Date: _____

_____
Director

_____
Director

_____
Director

_____
Director

MINUTES OF SPECIAL MEETING OF
THE BOARD OF DIRECTORS OF

_____

A special meeting of the Board of Directors of the Corporation was held on the date and at the time and place set forth in the written waiver of notice signed by the directors and attached to the minutes of this meeting.

The following were present, being all the directors of the Corporation:

_____   _____

_____   _____

The meeting was called to order and it was moved, seconded and unanimously carried that _____ act as Chairman and that _____ _____ act as Secretary.

The minutes of the last meeting of the Board of Directors which was held on _____, 20___ were read and approved by the Board.

Upon motion duly made, seconded and carried, the following resolution was adopted:

There being no further business to come before the meeting, upon motion duly made, seconded, and unanimously carried, it was adjourned.

_____
Secretary

Directors:

_____

_____

_____

_____

Change of Registered Agent and/or Registered Office

1.   The name of the corporation is:

2.   The street address of the current registered office is:

3.   The new address of the registered office is to be:

4.   The current registered agent is:

5.   The new registered agent is:

6.   The street address of the registered office and the street address of the business address of the registered agent are identical.

7.   Such change was authorized by resolution duly adopted by the Board of Directors of the corporation or by an officer of the corporation so authorized by the board of directors.

_____
Secretary

Having been named as registered agent and to accept service of process for the above stated corporation at the place designated in this certificate, I hereby accept the appointment as registered agent and agree to act in this capacity. I further agree to comply with the provisions of all statutes relating to the proper and complete performance of my duties, and am familiar with and accept the obligations of my position as registered agent.

_____
Registered Agent

INDEX

Your #1 Source for Real World Legal Information...

SPHINX® PUBLISHING
A Division of Sourcebooks, Inc.®
- Written by lawyers
- Simple English explanation of the law
- Forms and instructions included

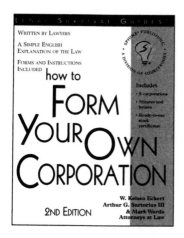 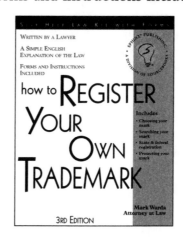 

HOW TO FORM YOUR OWN CORPORATION (2ND EDITION)

New business owners can save precious capital by forming their own corporations without the expense of a lawyer. This book includes a summary of the law, forms and instructions for forming a corporation in all 50 states and the District of Columbia.

208 pages; $19.95;
ISBN 1-57071-227-1

HOW TO REGISTER YOUR OWN TRADEMARK, 3RD ED.

Explains how to make a good choice of a mark and how to search the trademark office's new online database. It includes all the forms necessary to register and renew a trademark along with samples to guide you. Also discusses developing laws of Internet domain.

192 pages; $19.95;
ISBN 1-57248-104-8

HOW TO FORM A LIMITED LIABILITY COMPANY

Everything you need to start the newest form of doing business. Limited liability companies combine the protection of a corporation with the tax benefits of a partnership. Includes forms and instructions for forming an LLC in all 50 states, with state-by-state law summaries.

192 pages; $19.95;
ISBN 1-57248-083-1

See the following order form for books written specifically for California, Florida, Georgia, Illinois, Massachusetts, Michigan, Minnesota, New York, North Carolina, Pennsylvania, and Texas! *Coming soon—Ohio and New Jersey!*

What our customers say about our books:

"It couldn't be more clear for the lay person." —R.D.

"I want you to know I really appreciate your book. It has saved me a lot of time and money." —L.T.

"Your real estate contracts book has saved me nearly $12,000.00 in closing costs over the past year." —A.B.

"...many of the legal questions that I have had over the years were answered clearly and concisely through your plain English interpretation of the law." —C.E.H.

"If there weren't people out there like you I'd be lost. You have the best books of this type out there." —S.B.

"...your forms and directions are easy to follow." —C.V.M.

Sphinx Publishing's Legal Survival Guides
are directly available from the Sourcebooks, Inc., or from your local bookstores.
For credit card orders call 1–800–43–BRIGHT, write P.O. Box 4410, Naperville, IL 60567-4410,
or fax 630-961-2168

SPHINX® PUBLISHING'S NATIONAL TITLES

Valid in All 50 States

LEGAL SURVIVAL IN BUSINESS

How to Form a Limited Liability Company	$19.95
How to Form Your Own Corporation (2E)	$19.95
How to Form Your Own Partnership	$19.95
How to Register Your Own Copyright (2E)	$19.95
How to Register Your Own Trademark (3E)	$19.95
Most Valuable Business Legal Forms You'll Ever Need (2E)	$19.95
Most Valuable Corporate Forms You'll Ever Need (2E)	$24.95
Software Law (with diskette)	$29.95

LEGAL SURVIVAL IN COURT

Crime Victim's Guide to Justice	$19.95
Debtors' Rights (3E)	$12.95
Defend Yourself against Criminal Charges	$19.95
Grandparents' Rights (2E)	$19.95
Help Your Lawyer Win Your Case (2E)	$12.95
Jurors' Rights (2E)	$9.95
Legal Malpractice and Other Claims against Your Lawyer	$18.95
Legal Research Made Easy (2E)	$14.95
Simple Ways to Protect Yourself from Lawsuits	$24.95
Victims' Rights	$12.95
Winning Your Personal Injury Claim	$19.95

LEGAL SURVIVAL IN REAL ESTATE

How to Buy a Condominium or Townhome	$16.95
How to Negotiate Real Estate Contracts (3E)	$16.95
How to Negotiate Real Estate Leases (3E)	$16.95
Successful Real Estate Brokerage Management	$19.95

LEGAL SURVIVAL IN PERSONAL AFFAIRS

Your Right to Child Custody, Visitation and Support	$19.95
The Nanny and Domestic Help Legal Kit	$19.95
How to File Your Own Bankruptcy (4E)	$19.95
How to File Your Own Divorce (3E)	$19.95
How to Make Your Own Will	$12.95
How to Write Your Own Living Will	$9.95
How to Write Your Own Premarital Agreement (2E)	$19.95
How to Win Your Unemployment Compensation Claim	$19.95
Living Trusts and Simple Ways to Avoid Probate (2E)	$19.95
Neighbor v. Neighbor (2E)	$12.95
The Power of Attorney Handbook (3E)	$19.95
Simple Ways to Protect Yourself from Lawsuits	$24.95
Social Security Benefits Handbook (2E)	$14.95
Unmarried Parents' Rights	$19.95
U.S.A. Immigration Guide (3E)	$19.95
Guia de Inmigracion a Estados Unidos (2E)	$19.95

Legal Survival Guides are directly available from Sourcebooks, Inc., or from your local bookstores.

*For credit card orders call 1–800–43–BRIGHT, write P.O. Box 4410, Naperville, IL 60567-4410
or fax 630-961-2168*

SPHINX® PUBLISHING ORDER FORM

BILL TO:	SHIP TO:

Phone #	Terms	F.O.B. Chicago, IL	Ship Date

Charge my: ☐ VISA ☐ MasterCard ☐ American Express

☐ **Money Order or Personal Check**

Credit Card Number

Expiration Date

Qty	ISBN	Title	Retail	Ext.
		SPHINX PUBLISHING NATIONAL TITLES		
	1-57071-166-6	Crime Victim's Guide to Justice	$19.95	
	1-57071-342-1	Debtors' Rights (3E)	$12.95	
	1-57071-162-3	Defend Yourself against Criminal Charges	$19.95	
	1-57248-082-3	Grandparents' Rights (2E)	$19.95	
	1-57248-087-4	Guia de Inmigracion a Estados Unidos (2E)	$19.95	
	1-57248-103-X	Help Your Lawyer Win Your Case (2E)	$12.95	
	1-57071-164-X	How to Buy a Condominium or Townhome	$16.95	
	1-57071-223-9	How to File Your Own Bankruptcy (4E)	$19.95	
	1-57071-224-7	How to File Your Own Divorce (3E)	$19.95	
	1-57248-083-1	How to Form a Limited Liability Company	$19.95	
	1-57248-100-5	How to Form a DE Corporation from Any State	$19.95	
	1-57248-101-3	How to Form a NV Corporation from Any State	$19.95	
	1-57248-099-8	How to Form a Nonprofit Corporation	$24.95	
	1-57071-227-1	How to Form Your Own Corporation (2E)	$19.95	
	1-57071-343-X	How to Form Your Own Partnership	$19.95	
	1-57071-228-X	How to Make Your Own Will	$12.95	
	1-57071-331-6	How to Negotiate Real Estate Contracts (3E)	$16.95	
	1-57071-332-4	How to Negotiate Real Estate Leases (3E)	$16.95	
	1-57071-225-5	How to Register Your Own Copyright (2E)	$19.95	
	1-57248-104-8	How to Register Your Own Trademark (3E)	$19.95	
	1-57071-349-9	How to Win Your Unemployment Compensation Claim	$19.95	
	1-57071-167-4	How to Write Your Own Living Will	$9.95	
	1-57071-344-8	How to Write Your Own Premarital Agreement (2E)	$19.95	
	1-57071-333-2	Jurors' Rights (2E)	$9.95	
	1-57248-032-7	Legal Malpractice and Other Claims against...	$18.95	
	1-57071-400-2	Legal Research Made Easy (2E)	$14.95	
	1-57071-336-7	Living Trusts and Simple Ways to Avoid Probate (2E)	$19.95	
	1-57071-345-6	Most Valuable Bus. Legal Forms You'll Ever Need (2E)	$19.95	
	1-57071-346-4	Most Valuable Corporate Forms You'll Ever Need (2E)	$24.95	

Qty	ISBN	Title	Retail	Ext.
	1-57248-089-0	Neighbor v. Neighbor (2E)	$12.95	
	1-57071-348-0	The Power of Attorney Handbook (3E)	$19.95	
	1-57248-020-3	Simple Ways to Protect Yourself from Lawsuits	$24.95	
	1-57071-337-5	Social Security Benefits Handbook (2E)	$14.95	
	1-57071-163-1	Software Law (w/diskette)	$29.95	
	0-913825-86-7	Successful Real Estate Brokerage Mgmt.	$19.95	
	1-57248-098-X	The Nanny and Domestic Help Legal Kit	$19.95	
	1-57071-399-5	Unmarried Parents' Rights	$19.95	
	1-57071-354-5	U.S.A. Immigration Guide (3E)	$19.95	
	0-913825-82-4	Victims' Rights	$12.95	
	1-57071-165-8	Winning Your Personal Injury Claim	$19.95	
	1-57248-097-1	Your Right to Child Custody, Visitation and Support	$19.95	
		CALIFORNIA TITLES		
	1-57071-360-X	CA Power of Attorney Handbook	$12.95	
	1-57071-355-3	How to File for Divorce in CA	$19.95	
	1-57071-356-1	How to Make a CA Will	$12.95	
	1-57071-408-8	How to Probate an Estate in CA	$19.95	
	1-57071-357-X	How to Start a Business in CA	$16.95	
	1-57071-358-8	How to Win in Small Claims Court in CA	$14.95	
	1-57071-359-6	Landlords' Rights and Duties in CA	$19.95	
		FLORIDA TITLES		
	1-57071-363-4	Florida Power of Attorney Handbook (2E)	$12.95	
	1-57248-093-9	How to File for Divorce in FL (6E)	$21.95	
	1-57248-086-0	How to Form a Limited Liability Co. in FL	$19.95	
	1-57071-401-0	How to Form a Partnership in FL	$19.95	
	1-57071-380-4	How to Form a Corporation in FL (4E)	$19.95	
	1-57071-361-8	How to Make a FL Will (5E)	$12.95	
	1-57248-088-2	How to Modify Your FL Divorce Judgment (4E)	$22.95	

Form Continued on Following Page   **SUBTOTAL**

To order, call Sourcebooks at 1-800-43-BRIGHT or FAX (630)961-2168 (Bookstores, libraries, wholesalers—please call for discount)

SPHINX® PUBLISHING ORDER FORM

Qty	ISBN	Title	Retail	Ext.
		FLORIDA TITLES (CONT'D)		
___	1-57071-364-2	How to Probate an Estate in FL (3E)	$24.95	___
___	1-57248-081-5	How to Start a Business in FL (5E)	$16.95	___
___	1-57071-362-6	How to Win in Small Claims Court in FL (6E)	$14.95	___
___	1-57071-335-9	Landlords' Rights and Duties in FL (7E)	$19.95	___
___	1-57071-334-0	Land Trusts in FL (5E)	$24.95	___
___	0-913825-73-5	Women's Legal Rights in FL	$19.95	___
		GEORGIA TITLES		
___	1-57071-376-6	How to File for Divorce in GA (3E)	$19.95	___
___	1-57248-075-0	How to Make a GA Will (3E)	$12.95	___
___	1-57248-076-9	How to Start a Business in Georgia (3E)	$16.95	___
		ILLINOIS TITLES		
___	1-57071-405-3	How to File for Divorce in IL (2E)	$19.95	___
___	1-57071-415-0	How to Make an IL Will (2E)	$12.95	___
___	1-57071-416-9	How to Start a Business in IL (2E)	$16.95	___
___	1-57248-078-5	Landlords' Rights & Duties in IL	$19.95	___
		MASSACHUSETTS TITLES		
___	1-57071-329-4	How to File for Divorce in MA (2E)	$19.95	___
___	1-57248-108-0	How to Make a MA Will (2E)	$12.95	___
___	1-57248-109-9	How to Probate an Estate in MA (2E)	$19.95	___
___	1-57248-106-4	How to Start a Business in MA (2E)	$16.95	___
___	1-57248-107-2	Landlords' Rights and Duties in MA (2E)	$19.95	___
		MICHIGAN TITLES		
___	1-57071-409-6	How to File for Divorce in MI (2E)	$19.95	___
___	1-57248-077-7	How to Make a MI Will (2E)	$12.95	___
___	1-57071-407-X	How to Start a Business in MI (2E)	$16.95	___
		MINNESOTA TITLES		
___	1-57248-039-4	How to File for Divorce in MN	$19.95	___
___	1-57248-040-8	How to Form a Simple Corporation in MN	$19.95	___
___	1-57248-037-8	How to Make a MN Will	$9.95	___
___	1-57248-038-6	How to Start a Business in MN	$16.95	___
		NEW YORK TITLES		
___	1-57071-184-4	How to File for Divorce in NY	$19.95	___
___	1-57248-105-6	How to Form a Corporation in NY	$19.95	___

Qty	ISBN	Title	Retail	Ext.
		NEW YORK TITLES (CONT'D)		
___	1-57248-095-5	How to Make a NY Will (2E)	$12.95	___
___	1-57071-185-2	How to Start a Business in NY	$16.95	___
___	1-57071-187-9	How to Win in Small Claims Court in NY	$14.95	___
___	1-57071-186-0	Landlords' Rights and Duties in NY	$19.95	___
___	1-57071-188-7	New York Power of Attorney Handbook	$19.95	___
		NORTH CAROLINA TITLES		
___	1-57071-326-X	How to File for Divorce in NC (2E)	$19.95	___
___	1-57071-327-8	How to Make a NC Will (2E)	$12.95	___
___	1-57248-096-3	How to Start a Business in NC (2E)	$16.95	___
___	1-57248-091-2	Landlords' Rights & Duties in NC	$19.95	___
		OHIO TITLES		
___	1-57248-102-1	How to File for Divorce in OH	$19.95	___
		PENNSYLVANIA TITLES		
___	1-57071-177-1	How to File for Divorce in PA	$19.95	___
___	1-57248-094-7	How to Make a PA Will (2E)	$12.95	___
___	1-57248-112-9	How to Start a Business in PA (2E)	$16.95	___
___	1-57071-179-8	Landlords' Rights and Duties in PA	$19.95	___
		TEXAS TITLES		
___	1-57071-330-8	How to File for Divorce in TX (2E)	$19.95	___
___	1-57248-009-2	How to Form a Simple Corporation in TX	$19.95	___
___	1-57071-417-7	How to Make a TX Will (2E)	$12.95	___
___	1-57071-418-5	How to Probate an Estate in TX (2E)	$19.95	___
___	1-57071-365-0	How to Start a Business in TX (2E)	$16.95	___
___	1-57248-111-0	How to Win in Small Claims Court in TX (2E)	$14.95	___
___	1-57248-110-2	Landlords' Rights and Duties in TX (2E)	$19.95	___

SUBTOTAL THIS PAGE ___

SUBTOTAL PREVIOUS PAGE ___

Illinois residents add 6.75% sales tax

Florida residents add 6% state sales tax plus applicable discretionary surtax ___

Shipping— $4.00 for 1st book, $1.00 each additional ___

TOTAL ___